Betty Crocker's
HOLIDAY BAKING

PRENTICE HALL

New York   London   Toronto   Sydney   Tokyo   Singapore

PRENTICE HALL GENERAL REFERENCE
15 Columbus Circle
New York, New York, 10023

Library of Congress Cataloging-in-Publication Data

Crocker, Betty.
    [Holiday baking]
    Betty Crocker's holiday baking.
        p.   cm.
    Includes index.
    ISBN 0-671-86961-2
    1. Baking. 2. Holiday cookery. I. Title. II. Title: Holiday
baking.
    TX763.C764   1994
    641.7'1—dc20   92-46360
                                                        CIP

Designed by Levavi & Levavi, Inc.
Manufactured in the United States of America

10 9 8 7 6 5 4 3 2 1

First Edition

Front Cover: Raspberry-White Chocolate Cream Cake (page 37)

Back Cover: Deluxe Sugar Cookies (page 2); Stained-Glass Cookies (page 2); Santa Claus Cookies (page 13)

Contents

Letter from the Editors

The holidays are the perfect time for baking, when cookies, cakes, pies, breads and other treats are especially welcome. Beginning at Thanksgiving and continuing on through the new year, we all find many occasions for which baking is just the thing. From a Pumpkin Pie at Thanksgiving to Plum Pudding for Christmas dinner, cookies for holiday get-togethers and coffee cakes for brunch, there are many wonderful reasons to bake a variety of goodies and serve them fresh from the oven.

You'll find traditional recipes that will bring you cheer throughout the holiday season, such as classic brownies, chocolate chip cookies, sugar cookies, chocolate cake with fudge frosting and banana bread. And while we all have our favorite recipes, we are always eager for new ideas. For that reason, we have also collected recipes that will inspire you and add to your holiday festivities, such as Santa Claus Cookies, Peanut Butter Swirl Brownies, Raspberry-White Chocolate Cream Cake, Chocolate Angel Pie, Snowman Buns and Peppermint Cream Torte.

For new bakers, we've included helpful baking tips to ensure delicious results, as well as how to store baked goods. Beginners and old hands alike will appreciate information on freezing the holiday bounty for later use, as well as tips on mailing treats.

So, whether you want to bake a pecan pie for Thanksgiving, teach your children to make sugar cookie cutouts, create a stunning Bûche de Noël for Christmas Eve, craft a complete cookie chalet or explore new recipes for holiday treats, you'll find all the best ideas right here.

The Betty Crocker Editors

Introduction

START BAKING EARLY

"Next year I'm going to start in plenty of time." Sound familiar? Well, let this be the year to do it. Thanks to your freezer, you can prepare many of your holiday favorites well in advance and still preserve their fresh-baked quality. All it takes is a little know-how.

Guidelines for Freezing

- Make sure the temperature of your freezer is 0° or lower.
- Wrap food in moistureproof, vaporproof materials for maximum retention of flavor, moisture and nutrients. Before sealing, remove as much air from the package as possible.
- Label and date all packages.
- Don't turn your freezer into a holiday catchall. You'll want to leave enough room for your everyday freezing needs. Here are some start-ahead spans:

Breads (baked)—2 to 3 months
Cakes (unfrosted)—3 to 4 months
        (frosted)—2 to 3 months
Cookies (baked)—3 to 4 months
Fruitcakes (baked)—3 to 4 months
Pies (baked)—1 to 2 months
        (unbaked)—3 to 4 months
Steamed Puddings—3 to 4 months

Special Tips for Breads

- Before freezing, cool completely; wrap tightly in moistureproof, vaporproof material. Freezer bags will do the job too.
- Breads decorated with frostings and glazes can be frozen, but for the most attractive appearance, it's best to decorate just before giving or serving.
- Keep breads wrapped while thawing at room temperature.

Special Tips for Cookies

- Freeze frosted cookies uncovered until they are firm, then pack in a single layer in an airtight container lined with plastic wrap or aluminum foil. Seal the lining, close container, label and freeze.
- Cool unfrosted cookies thoroughly. Pack in layers in freezer container, separating layers with plastic wrap or foil. Then seal the lining, close container, label and freeze.
- Rolls or refrigerator cookie dough can be wrapped and frozen no longer than 6 months. When ready to bake, slice the frozen dough with a sharp knife.

Mail Early Too

There's no such thing as "too early" when it comes to mailing Christmas cookies. Label your package "Open Before Christmas" and think how much more the recipient will enjoy your thoughtfulness during the holidays. If you mail before the Christmas rush, your package will also reach its destination faster. Check the post office for delivery time estimates of the various mail classifications.

• Choose plain or lightly glazed bar cookies.
• Cut rolled cookies with rounded (not pointed or delicately shaped) cutters to avoid crumbling and breakage.
• Wrap cookies in pairs, back to back, and place them in a can, box or other sturdy container. (You'll find that cans with reusable plastic lids are particularly good choices.)
• Fill each container as full as practical, padding the top with crushed paper to prevent shaking and breakage.
• Pack containers in a foil-lined corrugated or fiberboard packing box. For filler, use crumpled newspapers, shredded paper or shredded polyethylene foam.
• Seal packing box with "strapping tape"; wrap tightly in heavy paper and seal with tape.
• Write address on the package or gummed label in large, legible print. Cover address with transparent tape to protect it.

BEST BAKING TIPS

Follow these helpful guides for your best baking results.

Cookies: Use a shiny cookie sheet at least 2 inches narrower and shorter than the oven. The sheet may be open on one to three sides. If a sheet with a nonstick coating is used, watch carefully—cookies may brown quickly. Follow manufacturer's directions as many suggest reducing the oven temperature by 25°. If cookie sheets are thin, consider using two cookie sheets (one on top of the other) for insulation. If cookie sheets are too thin, cookies can bake too rapidly and burn on the bottom.

Cakes: Shiny metal pans reflect heat away from the cake. They produce a tender, light-brown crust, and are preferred for baking cakes. Dark nonstick or glass baking pans should be used by following the manufacturer's directions. These pans readily absorb heat and a better result is often achieved if the baking temperature is reduced by 25°.

Pies: The right bakeware is the key to making the perfect pie. Choose heat-resistant glass pie plates or dull-finish (anodized) aluminum pans. Never use shiny pans—pie will have a soggy bottom crust. Nonstick pie pans can cause pastry to shrink excessively when baking one-crust pie shells. Be sure pastry is securely hooked over the edge of a nonstick pan.

Quick Breads: Use shiny pans and cookie sheets, which reflect heat, for golden, delicate and tender crusts on muffins, coffee cakes and nut breads. If pans with dark or nonstick coating are used, watch carefully so foods don't over-brown and follow manufacturer's directions, as many suggest reducing the oven temperature by 25°.

Yeast Breads: Use loaf pans of anodized aluminum, darkened metal or glass for bread with well-browned crusts. If pans with dark nonstick coating are used, watch carefully so bread doesn't overbrown. Follow manufacturer's directions, since reducing the oven temperature is often recommended.

STORING TIPS

Follow these tips for storing your holiday baking—see page 36 for storage tips on cakes.

Storing Cookies and Bars

- Keep different kinds of cookies and bars in separate containers to maintain the best flavor.
- Store crisp cookies loosely covered. If they become soft, heat in a 300° oven 3 to 5 minutes or until warm. (In humid weather, they'll keep best tightly covered.)
- Store soft cookies tightly covered. If replaced often, a piece of bread or apple in the container will help keep the cookies soft.
- Store brownies and bars in tightly covered containers, or leave them in the pan and cover tightly with foil.

Storing Pies

- Pies containing eggs should be refrigerated.
- Pie shells can be frozen unbaked or baked. Frozen unbaked shells will keep two months and baked shells four months. To thaw baked pie shells, unwrap and let stand at room temperature or heat in 350° oven about 6 minutes. Do not thaw unbaked shells; immediately bake after removing from freezer.
- Baked pies can be frozen. They are easiest to wrap if frozen uncovered, then wrapped tightly or placed in freezer plastic bags. Bake pies before freezing to prevent soggy crusts or possible texture breakdown of raw fruit. Frozen baked pies will keep up to four months.
- To serve frozen two-crust pies, unwrap and thaw at room temperature 1 hour. Heat in 375° oven on lowest rack for 35 to 40 minutes until warm.

Storing Nut Breads

- Grease only the bottoms of loaf pans for fruit or nut breads. Ungreased sides allow the batter to cling while rising during baking, which helps form a gently rounded top.
- Cool nut breads completely (preferably storing, tightly covered, twenty-four hours) before slicing to prevent crumbling. Cut with a sharp, thin-bladed knife, using a light sawing motion.

PRETTY CAKES AND PIES

Make your holiday cakes and pies special with these hints!

Frosting Two-Layer Cakes

Here's an easy way to frost a layer cake to get professional-looking results:

1. Lay strips of waxed paper along edge of cake plate. Brush loose crumbs away from cake layers; place one layer, rounded side down, on plate.
2. Spread about 1/3 cup frosting over top of layer to within about 1/4 inch of the edge. Place second layer, rounded side up, on top of first layer.
3. Coat the side of the cake with a very thin layer of frosting to seal in the crumbs. Frost the side of the cake in swirls, making a rim about 1/4 inch high above the top of the cake to make the top appear flat.
4. Spread remaining frosting on top, just to the built-up rim. Remove waxed paper strips.

Pretty Pie Crusts

Use a cookie cutter or canapé cutter to create your own unique look with two-crust pies. Instead of cutting slits in top crust for the juices to bubble through, cut out a few shapes with a mini-cutter. Small cutouts can be overlapped to form a decorative edge. Or larger cutouts can be overlapped to form the top crust of a pie. (To keep the filling from bubbling out the edge of the pie, fold the edge of the lower pie crust up and over the cutouts, sealing the pastry and building up a high edge.)

Gingerbread Cookie Tree

1
Creative Cookies

Gingerbread Cookie Tree

This "tree" is an edible centerpiece that can be made from stars, hearts, fluted circles or rings. Ten cutters, ranging from 2 to 8¾ inches (increasing by ¾ inch from one size to the next) are required. Nested cookie-cutter sets are available in specialty shops, but homemade patterns work just as well.

2 recipes Gingerbread Cookies (page 4)
4 cups powdered sugar
1 teaspoon vanilla
4 to 5 tablespoons half-and-half
Assorted candies, if desired

Prepare and refrigerate recipes individually as directed. Heat oven to 350°. Lightly grease cookie sheet.

Roll half of 1 recipe of dough at a time ¼ inch thick on floured surface. Cut 3 cookies of each size with floured cutters or patterns. Place about 2 inches apart on cookie sheet. Bake large cookies 12 to 14 minutes and small cookies 8 to 10 minutes or until no indentation remains when touched. Cool slightly; remove from cookie sheet. Cool completely.

Beat powdered sugar, vanilla and half-and-half until smooth and of spreading consistency. Assemble tree on serving plate or foil-covered cardboard: Starting with largest cookies, stack cookies as frosted, or stack unfrosted cookies together with small dab of frosting in center of each. Let layers dry or hold cookies in place with bamboo skewers if necessary. Use remaining frosting to pipe "snow" on the tree with decorating bag. Decorate with assorted candies.

1 cookie tree (60 servings)

PER SERVING: Calories 235; Protein 3 g; Carbohydrate 49 g; Fat 3 g; Cholesterol 0 mg; Sodium 135 mg

Deluxe Sugar Cookies

Sugar Cookies offer a world of decorating opportunity and are a particular hit with children.

1½ cups powdered sugar
1 cup margarine or butter, softened
1 egg
1 teaspoon vanilla
½ teaspoon almond extract
2½ cups all-purpose flour
1 teaspoon baking soda
1 teaspoon cream of tartar

Mix powdered sugar, margarine, egg, vanilla and almond extract. Stir in flour, baking soda and cream of tartar. Cover and refrigerate at least 3 hours.

Heat oven to 375°. Divide dough into halves. Roll each half ³⁄₁₆ inch thick on lightly floured cloth-covered board. Cut into desired shapes with cookie cutters. Place on ungreased cookie sheet. Bake until edges are light brown, 7 to 8 minutes. Frost and decorate as desired.

about 5 dozen 2-inch cookies

STAINED-GLASS COOKIES: Before refrigerating, divide dough into halves. Divide 1 half into 3 to 5 parts. Tint each part with a different food color. Wrap each part and the plain dough separately in plastic wrap and refrigerate at least 3 hours. Roll plain dough ⅛ inch thick on lightly floured cloth-covered board. Cut with bell, star, tree and other decorative cookie cutters. Place on ungreased cookie sheet. Roll tinted doughs ⅛ inch thick; cut out different shapes to fit on each cookie. Heat oven to 375°. Bake until golden, 7 to 8 minutes.

PER SERVING: Calories 60; Protein 0 g; Carbohydrate 7 g; Fat 3 g; Cholesterol 5 mg; Sodium 55 mg

Holiday Cutouts

Prepare dough as directed for Deluxe Sugar Cookies (left), or Merry Christmas Molasses Cookies (page 4) or light ginger cookies. After rolling out dough, cut into assorted shapes with cookie cutters or cut around patterns traced from storybook illustrations. If desired, cut small appliqués of dough and press on cookies. Cookies can be decorated before baking with Baked-On Decorators' Frosting (below) or afterward with Creamy Decorators' Frosting (below). Use colored sugars, sprinkles and nonpareils.

To outline designs on baked cookies, place frosting in a decorators' tube. Or cut off a tiny corner of a #10 envelope or small strong plastic bag. Fill with about ⅓ cup frosting at a time. Ready-to-use frosting tubes can also be used.

To hang cookies on a Christmas tree or wreath, loop a piece of string and press ends into underside of each cookie before baking or use a drinking straw to poke a hole.

Baked-On Decorators' Frosting

Mix ⅓ cup all-purpose flour and ⅓ cup margarine or butter, softened, until smooth. Stir in 1½ teaspoons hot water and, if desired, 2 or 3 drops food color. Place in decorators' tube with #3 writing tip. Outline, write or make designs on unbaked rolled cookies. Bake cookies as directed in recipe. Cool; store carefully, separating layers of cookies with waxed paper.

enough for 2 to 3 dozen cookies

Creamy Decorators' Frosting

Beat 1 cup powdered sugar, ½ teaspoon vanilla and about 1 tablespoon water or half-and-half until smooth and of spreading consistency. Tint with food color if desired.

enough for 3 to 5 dozen cookies

PER SERVING: Calories 80; Protein 1 g; Carbohydrate 10 g; Fat 4 g; Cholesterol 5 mg; Sodium 65 mg

Holiday Cutouts

Merry Christmas Molasses Cookies

⅔ cup packed brown sugar
⅔ cup shortening
1⅓ cups molasses
5½ cups all-purpose flour
2 teaspoons baking soda
2 teaspoons ground ginger
1 teaspoon salt
4 teaspoons ground cinnamon
2 eggs

Mix brown sugar, shortening and molasses. Stir in remaining ingredients. Cover and refrigerate at least 1 hour.

Heat oven to 375°. Roll dough ¼ inch thick on lightly floured cloth-covered board. Cut into desired shapes with cookie cutters. Place about 1 inch apart on lightly greased cookie sheet. Bake until no indentation remains when touched, 7 to 8 minutes; cool. Frost and decorate as desired.   **about 5 dozen 3-inch cookies**

PER SERVING: Calories 100; Protein 1 g; Carbohydrate 16 g; Fat 3 g; Cholesterol 5 mg; Sodium 70 mg

Gingerbread Cookies

1 cup packed brown sugar
⅓ cup shortening
1½ cups dark molasses
⅔ cup cold water
7 cups all-purpose flour
2 teaspoons baking soda
2 teaspoons ground ginger
1 teaspoon salt
1 teaspoon ground allspice
1 teaspoon ground cloves
1 teaspoon ground cinnamon
Creamy Frosting (below)

Mix brown sugar, shortening, molasses and water in large bowl. Stir in remaining ingredients except Creamy Frosting. Cover and refrigerate about 2 hours or until firm.

Heat oven to 350°. Lightly grease cookie sheet. Roll one-fourth of dough at a time ¼ inch thick on floured surface. Cut with floured gingerbread cookie cutter or other favorite shaped cutter. Place about 2 inches apart on cookie sheet. Bake 10 to 12 minutes or until almost no indentation remains when touched in center. Remove from cookie sheet. Cool completely. Prepare Creamy Frosting and spread on cookies.

about 2½ dozen 5-inch gingerbread cookies or about 5 dozen 2½-inch cookies

Creamy Frosting

4 cups powdered sugar
5 tablespoons half-and-half
1 teaspoon vanilla
Food color, if desired

Mix all ingredients until smooth.

PER SERVING: Calories 270; Protein 3 g; Carbohydrate 57 g; Fat 3 g; Cholesterol 0 mg; Sodium 140 mg

Move Over Chocolate Chips!

Today, instead of chocolate chips, you can stir many other exciting treats into cookies for a fun change of pace. Mix and match the plain or chocolate cookie recipes with any of these cookie stir-ins for great results.

Stir-in Morsels

CANDY	Plain Cookies	Choco-late Cookies
Chocolate mint wafers, chopped	X	X
Chocolate toffee crunch thin candies	X	X
Milk chocolate–covered raisins	X	X
Miniature pastel-colored mint candy kisses	X	X
Multicolored bite-size licorice candy	X	
Fruit-flavored gumdrops, cut up	X	
Chocolate-covered peanuts, coarsely chopped	X	X
Malted milk balls, coarsely chopped	X	X
Candy coated chocolate chips	X	X
Vanilla milk chips		X
NUTS		
Honey-roasted nuts, coarsely chopped		X
Pistachio nuts, chopped	X	X
Macadamia nuts, coarsely chopped	X	X
Trail mix combinations (nuts and raisins)	X	X

Moravian Ginger Cookies

⅓ cup molasses
¼ cup shortening
2 tablespoons packed brown sugar
1¼ cups all-purpose or whole wheat flour
¼ teaspoon salt
¼ teaspoon baking soda
¼ teaspoon baking powder
¼ teaspoon ground cinnamon
¼ teaspoon ground ginger
¼ teaspoon ground cloves
Dash of ground nutmeg
Dash of ground allspice
Easy Creamy Frosting (below)

Mix molasses, shortening and brown sugar in large bowl. Stir in remaining ingredients except Easy Creamy Frosting. Cover and refrigerate about 4 hours or until firm.

Heat oven to 375°. Roll half of dough at a time ⅛ inch thick or paper-thin on floured cloth-covered surface. Cut into 3-inch rounds with floured cutter. Place about ½ inch apart on ungreased cookie sheet. Bake ⅛-inch-thick cookies about 8 minutes, paper-thin cookies about 5 minutes or until light brown. Immediately remove from cookie sheet. Cool completely. Prepare Easy Creamy Frosting and spread on cookies.

**about 1 dozen ⅛-inch-thick cookies
or about 1½ dozen paper-thin cookies**

Easy Creamy Frosting

1 cup powdered sugar
½ teaspoon vanilla
1 to 2 tablespoons half-and-half

Mix ingredients until of spreading consistency.

PER SERVING: Calories 170; Protein 1 g; Carbohydrate 29 g; Fat 5 g; Cholesterol 0 mg; Sodium 75 mg

Hungarian Poppy Seed Cookies

Lemon peel, clove and poppy seed often flavor Eastern European cookies. Look for commercially prepared poppy seed filling next to canned pie fillings at the supermarket.

½ cup margarine or butter
¼ cup granulated sugar
1 teaspoon grated lemon peel
1 egg
1¼ cups all-purpose flour
½ teaspoon baking soda
¼ teaspoon ground cloves
¾ cup poppy seed filling
Powdered sugar

Beat margarine and granulated sugar in large bowl until light and fluffy. Beat in lemon peel and egg. Stir in flour, baking soda and cloves. Roll dough between pieces of waxed paper into ¼-inch-thick rectangle, 12 × 10 inches. Refrigerate 30 minutes or until firm.

Heat oven to 350°. Grease cookie sheet. Remove waxed paper from one side of dough. Spread poppy seed filling to within ¼ inch of edges. Roll up tightly, beginning at 12-inch side, peeling off waxed paper as dough is rolled. Pinch edge of dough to seal well. Cut dough into ½-inch slices. Place on cookie sheet about 1 inch apart. Bake 10 to 12 minutes or until edges are light brown. Cool slightly; remove from cookie sheet. Sprinkle with powdered sugar. **about 3 dozen cookies**

PER SERVING: Calories 75; Protein 1 g; Carbohydrate 7 g; Fat 5 g; Cholesterol 5 mg; Sodium 50 mg

Almond-filled Crescents

1 cup powdered sugar
1 cup whipping (heavy) cream
2 eggs
3¾ cups all-purpose flour
1 teaspoon baking powder
½ teaspoon salt
1 can (8 ounces) almond paste
¾ cup margarine or butter, softened
Glaze (below)

Mix powdered sugar, whipping cream and eggs in large bowl. Stir in flour, baking powder and salt. (Dough will be stiff.) Cover and refrigerate about 1 hour or until firm.

Heat oven to 375°. Break almond paste into small pieces in medium bowl; add margarine. Beat on low speed until blended. Beat on high speed until fluffy (tiny bits of almond paste will remain).

Roll one-fourth of dough at a time into 10-inch circle on lightly floured surface. Spread one-fourth of almond paste mixture (about ½ cup) over circle. Cut into 12 wedges. Roll up, beginning at rounded edge. Place on ungreased cookie sheet with points underneath. Curve cookies to form crescents. Repeat with remaining dough and almond paste mixture. Bake 14 to 16 minutes or until golden brown. Remove from cookie sheet. Cool completely. Prepare Glaze and drizzle on crescents.

4 dozen crescents

Glaze

1 cup powdered sugar
6 to 7 teaspoons milk

Mix until smooth and of desired consistency.

PER SERVING: Calories 120; Protein 2 g; Carbohydrate 15 g; Fat 6 g; Cholesterol 15 mg; Sodium 70 mg

Butterscotch Shortbread

If you prefer shortbread cutouts, use a 2-inch cookie cutter.

½ **cup margarine or butter, softened**
½ **cup shortening**
½ **cup packed brown sugar**
¼ **cup granulated sugar**
2¼ **cups all-purpose flour**
1 **teaspoon salt**

Heat oven to 300°. Mix margarine, shortening and sugars in large bowl. Stir in flour and salt. (Dough will be dry and crumbly. Use hands to mix completely.) Roll dough into rectangle, 15 × 7½ inches, on lightly floured surface. Cut into 1½-inch squares. Place about 1 inch apart on ungreased cookie sheet. Bake about 25 minutes or until set. (These cookies brown very little and the shape does not change.) Remove from cookie sheet.   **about 4 dozen cookies**

PER SERVING: Calories 70; Protein 0 g; Carbohydrate 8 g; Fat 4 g; Cholesterol 0 mg; Sodium 70 mg

Chocolate Shortbread

As an alternative to the frosted spiderweb design described at right, drizzle straight lines of chocolate across the white frosting; draw a wooden pick across the lines, alternating directions.

2 **cups powdered sugar**
1½ **cups margarine or butter**
3 **cups all-purpose flour**
¾ **cup cocoa**
2 **teaspoons vanilla**
4 **ounces semisweet chocolate, melted and cooled**
½ **teaspoon shortening**
Vanilla Frosting (right)

Heat oven to 325°. Beat powdered sugar and margarine in large bowl until light and fluffy. Stir in flour, cocoa and vanilla.

Roll half of dough at a time ½ inch thick on lightly floured surface. Cut into 3-inch rounds. Place 2 inches apart on ungreased cookie sheet. Bake 9 to 11 inches or until firm. (Do not let cookies get dark brown.) Remove from cookie sheet. Cool completely.

Mix chocolate and shortening until smooth. Prepare Vanilla Frosting and spread each cookie with about 1 teaspoon. Immediately drizzle chocolate mixture on frosting making 3 concentric circles. Starting at center, draw a toothpick 5 to 6 times through chocolate circles to make spiderweb design. Let stand until chocolate is firm.   **about 4 dozen cookies**

Vanilla Frosting

3 **cups powdered sugar**
⅓ **cup margarine or butter, softened**
1½ **teaspoons vanilla**
About 2 tablespoons milk

Mix powdered sugar and margarine in medium bowl. Stir in vanilla and milk. Beat until smooth and of spreading consistency.

PER SERVING: Calories 160; Protein 1 g; Carbohydrate 21 g; Fat 8 g; Cholesterol 0 mg; Sodium 80 mg

Cookie Chalet

Equipment
Grid paper for enlarging patterns
Heavy paper for patterns
1 or 2 cookie sheets (15½ × 12 inches)
Stockinet-covered rolling pin
Small sharp knife and scissors
Waxed paper
Small spatula
Decorators' tube or envelope cone
#3 and #10 tips for decorators' tube
Tray (base for chalet)

Preparation
1. Prepare Merry Christmas Molasses Cookies dough (page 4) as directed—except use light molasses, omit cinnamon and decrease baking soda to 1 teaspoon. Refrigerate at least 1 hour. Enlarge patterns according to scale (see Pattern Plan, page 9) and cut from heavy paper.

2. Roll 2 cups dough into rectangle, 15 × 10 inches, on lightly greased cookie sheet with floured stockinet-covered rolling pin. (If cookie sheet slips while rolling, place dampened towel underneath.) Heat oven to 375°. Place patterns on rectangle as shown in Diagram A. (The dough will expand during baking, so be sure to place the patterns at least ½ inch apart.) Cut around patterns with sharp knife; remove and reserve excess dough. Make slight marks with knife to indicate position of doors and windows. Bake until no indentation remains when touched, 5 to 6 minutes for small pieces, about 10 minutes for large pieces. Cool large pieces 1 to 2 minutes; remove to wire rack.

3. Repeat Step 2 except place patterns on rectangle as shown in Diagram B. Before baking, cut ⅜-inch-wide slot 1½ inches down from top of half of the trees; cut ⅜-inch-wide slot 1¾ inches up from bottom of remaining trees. After baking, while cookie trees are warm, insert bottom slot of one tree into top slot of another; repeat.

4. Roll about ½ cup dough 1/16 inch thick into rectangle, about 8 × 6 inches, on lightly greased cookie sheet. Cut into 2 rectangles, each 7 × 2¼ inches, for the shutters as shown in Diagram C; reserve excess dough. Cut each rectangle into seven 1-inch strips. Remove every other strip, leaving 8 shutters. Bake shutters 5 to 6 minutes.

5. Press remaining dough and the reserved dough into a ball (about 2 cups); knead in ⅓ cup cocoa. Roll 1½ cups cocoa dough into rectangle, 15 × 8 inches, on lightly greased cookie sheet. Cut 2 roof pieces as shown in Diagram D. Remove and reserve excess dough. Bake roof pieces about 10 minutes. Cool 1 to 2 minutes.

6. Roll all remaining dough 1/16 inch thick into square, about 9 × 9 inches, on lightly greased cookie sheet. Cut into 20 strips, each 9 × ⅜ inch, for trim. Remove every other strip, leaving 10 trim strips on cookie sheet. Bake trim strips 6 to 8 minutes.

7. Roll remaining dough about ⅛ inch thick; cut to form stones for path. Cut additional trees if desired. Bake 5 to 6 minutes.

Trimming and Construction
1. Flatten 8 small red gumdrops and 8 small green gumdrops with rolling pin between 2 sheets of waxed paper. Cut 16 heart designs from red gumdrops with sharp knife or scissors. (Dip knife or scissors into hot water for easier cutting.) Cut accent designs from green gumdrops.

2. Prepare 1 package (7.2 ounces) fluffy white frosting mix as directed on package. Stir in 3 cups powdered sugar, ½ cup at a time, until thick and smooth. Keep covered.

3. Tint about ½ cup frosting with yellow food color. Frost door area and shutters using small spatula. Press gumdrop appliqués into position on shutters.

4. Place about ⅓ cup frosting in decorators' tube with #3 tip or pipe lattice design for window panes on sides of house. Spread a strip of frosting on back of each shutter; press into position around panes.

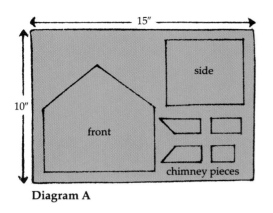

Diagram A

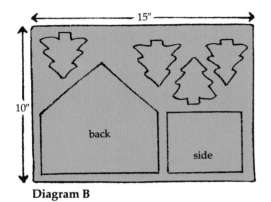

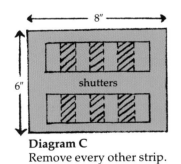

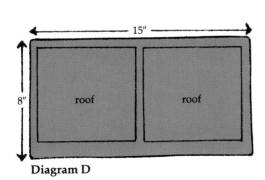

Diagram B

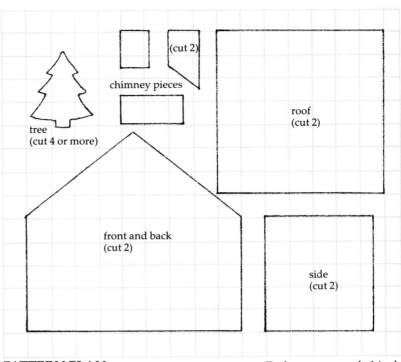

side

chimney pieces

(cut 2)

chimney pieces

roof
(cut 2)

tree
(cut 4 or more)

front and back
(cut 2)

side
(cut 2)

PATTERN PLAN Each square equals 1 inch.

A 3-inch tree-shaped cookie cutter can be used instead of pattern.

Diagram C
Remove every other strip.

shutters

Diagram D

roof

roof

Details for front of chalet. Repeat window treatment on sides and back; repeat attic trim on back if desired.

5. Mix remaining frosting and ¼ cup cocoa. Keep covered. If frosting becomes too thick, stir in a few drops of water. Attach 9-inch strips to top and bottom of front and back of house, using cocoa frosting for "concrete." Cut strips to fit along bottom of each side of house and below eaves if desired; attach with cocoa frosting. Cut strips for attic trim at a slant with sharp knife; cut strips for door trim. Attach with cocoa frosting.

6. Place remaining cocoa frosting in decorators' tube with #10 tip. Pipe strip above and below window lattice. Pipe ½-inch strip of frosting on inside vertical edges of back of house. Using a tray for the base, place back of house in vertical position on tray; press side pieces of house into frosting, making sure corners are square. Pipe cocoa frosting on inside vertical edges of front of house; press to front sides of house. Pipe frosting along inside vertical seam lines for reinforcement. Let set about 30 minutes. (Cans or bottles can be used to hold house in place.)

7. Pipe frosting generously along top edges of front and back of house. Place roof pieces on top, making sure peaks meet in center.

8. Pipe frosting on inside vertical edges of 2 slanted chimney pieces. Press side pieces of chimney into frosting to form "box." Hold a few minutes until set; let dry. Pipe frosting on bottom edges of chimney; place on roof. Pipe any remaining frosting into seams as needed.

9. Arrange trees and path around house as desired. Sprinkle trees, path, house and tray lightly with powdered sugar. **60 servings**

PER SERVING: Calories 95; Protein 1 g; Carbohydrate 16 g; Fat 3 g; Cholesterol 5 mg; Sodium 55 mg

Insert bottom slot of one tree into top slot of another; trees will stand upright.

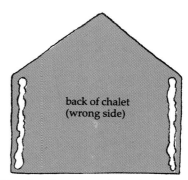

Pipe frosting on vertical edges on *inside* of back of chalet.

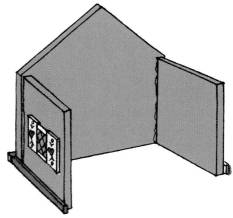

When pressing side pieces to frosting, make sure corners are square.

Pipe frosting on vertical edges on *inside* of front of chalet. Press front piece to sides.

Cookie Chalet

Peachy Pinwheels

For the freshest nutmeg flavor, grate your own nutmeg.

1 cup finely chopped dried peaches
¾ cup water
½ cup sugar
½ teaspoon ground nutmeg
½ cup margarine or butter, softened
¼ cup shortening
1 cup sugar
2 eggs
1 teaspoon vanilla
2½ cups all-purpose flour
1 teaspoon baking powder
¼ teaspoon salt

Mix peaches, water, ½ cup sugar and the nutmeg in 1-quart saucepan. Heat to boiling; reduce heat. Cover and simmer about 35 minutes or until peaches are tender and water is almost absorbed; cool slightly. Mash with fork.

Mix margarine, shortening, 1 cup sugar, the eggs and vanilla. Stir in remaining ingredients. Cover and refrigerate at least 1 hour.

Divide dough in half. Roll each half into rectangle, 11 × 7 inches, on floured surface. Spread half of the peach mixture to within ½ inch of edges of each rectangle. Roll up tightly, beginning at long side. Pinch to seal. Wrap and refrigerate at least 4 hours or until firm.

Heat oven to 375°. Cut roll into ¼-inch slices. Place on ungreased cookie sheet. Bake about 10 minutes or until light brown; cool.

about 5 dozen cookies

PER SERVING: Calories 75; Protein 1 g; Carbohydrate 11 g; Fat 3 g; Cholesterol 10 mg; Sodium 40 mg

Peppernuts

These cookies are also very nice rolled in powdered sugar.

¾ cup packed brown sugar
½ cup shortening
½ cup molasses
1 egg
1 tablespoon hot water
3 drops anise oil
3⅓ cups all-purpose flour
½ teaspoon baking soda
½ teaspoon ground cinnamon
½ teaspoon ground cloves
¼ teaspoon salt
⅛ teaspoon white pepper

Mix brown sugar, shortening, molasses, egg, water and anise oil. Stir in remaining ingredients. Knead dough until of right consistency for molding. Heat oven to 350°. Shape dough into ¾-inch balls. Place about 1 inch apart on ungreased cookie sheet. Bake until bottoms are golden brown, about 12 minutes.

about 8 dozen cookies

NOTE: For the traditionally hard Peppernuts, store in airtight container. For softer cookies, store with a slice of apple in airtight container; replace apple frequently.

PER SERVING: Calories 30; Protein 0 g; Carbohydrate 6 g; Fat 1 g; Cholesterol 5 mg; Sodium 10 mg

Santa Claus Cookies

1 cup granulated sugar
½ cup shortening
2 tablespoons milk
1 teaspoon grated lemon peel
1 egg
2 cups all-purpose flour
1 teaspoon baking powder
½ teaspoon baking soda
½ teaspoon salt
Creamy Frosting (below)
Miniature marshmallows
Red sugar
Currants or semisweet chocolate chips
Red cinnamon candies
Shredded coconut

Mix granulated sugar, shortening, milk, lemon peel and egg. Stir in flour, baking powder, baking soda and salt. Heat oven to 400°. Shape dough into 1¼-inch balls. Place about 2 inches apart on ungreased cookie sheet; flatten each to about 2½-inch diameter with greased bottom of glass dipped in sugar. Bake until edges are light brown, 8 to 10 minutes; cool.

Spread cookie with small amount of Creamy Frosting. Press on miniature marshmallow for tassel of cap. Sprinkle top third of cookie with red sugar. Press 2 currants for eyes and red cinnamon candy for nose into center third. Sprinkle bottom third with coconut for beard. Frost and decorate each cookie before starting another.   **about 1½ dozen cookies**

Creamy Frosting

1½ cups powdered sugar
½ teaspoon vanilla
2 to 3 tablespoons water

Mix all ingredients until of desired consistency.

SANTA CLAUS COOKIE POPS: After shaping dough into balls, insert wooden ice-cream sticks halfway into balls; continue as directed.

PER SERVING: Calories 220; Protein 2 g; Carbohydrate 36 g; Fat 0 g; Cholesterol 10 mg; Sodium 115 mg

Almond Bonbons

In the place of almond paste, try wrapping this dough around nuts, chocolate chunks or dried fruit. Tint the glaze for a more festive look and decorate as desired.

1½ cups all-purpose flour
½ cup margarine or butter, softened
⅓ cup powdered sugar
2 tablespoons milk
½ teaspoon vanilla
1 package (3½ ounces) almond paste
Glaze (below)
Sliced almonds, toasted if desired

Heat oven to 375°. Mix flour, margarine, powdered sugar, milk and vanilla in large bowl. Cut almond paste into ½-inch slices; cut each slice into fourths.

Shape 1-inch ball of dough around each piece of almond paste. Gently roll to form ball. Place about 1 inch apart on ungreased cookie sheet. Bake 10 to 12 minutes or until set and bottom is golden brown. Remove from cookie sheet. Cool completely. Prepare Glaze and dip in tops of cookies. Garnish with sliced almonds.

about 3 dozen cookies

Glaze

1 cup powdered sugar
½ teaspoon almond extract
4 to 5 teaspoons milk

Mix all ingredients until smooth and of desired consistency.

PER SERVING: Calories 80; Protein 1 g; Carbohydrate 10 g; Fat 4 g; Cholesterol 0 mg; Sodium 30 mg

Chocolate-Peppermint Refrigerator Cookies

1½ cups powdered sugar
1 cup margarine or butter, softened
1 egg
2⅔ cups all-purpose flour
¼ teaspoon salt
¼ cup cocoa
1 tablespoon milk
¼ cup finely crushed peppermint candy

Mix powdered sugar, margarine and egg in large bowl. Stir in flour and salt. Divide dough in half. Stir cocoa and milk into one half and peppermint candy into other half.

Shape chocolate dough into rectangle, 12 × 6½ inches, on waxed paper. Shape peppermint dough into roll, 12 inches long; place on chocolate dough. Wrap chocolate dough around peppermint dough using waxed paper to help lift. Press edges together. Wrap and refrigerate about 2 hours or until firm.

Heat oven to 375°. Cut rolls into ¼-inch slices. Place about 1 inch apart on ungreased cookie sheet. Bake 8 to 10 minutes or until set. Remove from cookie sheet.   **4 dozen cookies**

CHOCOLATE-WINTERGREEN REFRIGERATOR COOKIES: Omit peppermint candies. Stir ¼ cup chocolate shot, ¼ teaspoon wintergreen extract and 4 drops green food color into plain dough. Continue as directed.

PER SERVING: Calories 80; Protein 1 g; Carbohydrate 11 g; Fat 4 g; Cholesterol 5 mg; Sodium 60 mg

Springerle

From Germany comes this embossed Christmas cookie with centuries of tradition. A springerle rolling pin has recessed designs that make an imprint on the dough. The imprinted cookies are separated, then traditionally allowed to dry overnight, which helps set the design. We don't recommend air drying because the dough contains raw egg; if there isn't time to bake the cookies immediately, refrigerate (in a single layer, loosely covered) up to twenty-four hours. These richly flavored cookies are very hard—excellent for dunking.

1 cup sugar
2 eggs
2 cups all-purpose flour
2 teaspoons anise seed

Heat oven to 325°. Beat sugar and eggs in large bowl about 5 minutes or until thick and lemon colored. Stir in flour and anise seed.

Roll half of dough at a time ¼ inch thick on floured cloth-covered surface. Roll well-floured springerle rolling pin over dough to emboss with designs. Cut out cookies. Place about 1 inch apart on ungreased cookie sheet. Bake 12 to 15 minutes or until light brown. Immediately remove from cookie sheet.

about 3 dozen cookies

PER SERVING: Calories 50; Protein 1 g; Carbohydrate 11 g; Fat 0 g; Cholesterol 10 mg; Sodium 5 mg

Bottom: Springerle, Middle: Krumkake (page 16), Top: Pizzelles (page 16)

Pizzelles

These Italian cookies are wafer-thin and lightly flavored with anise. They are cooked in a hot pizzelle iron, also known as a cialde iron. If you work quickly, you can roll the hot cookie into a cylinder.

2 cups all-purpose flour
1 cup sugar
¾ cup margarine or butter, melted and cooled
1 tablespoon anise extract or vanilla
4 eggs, slightly beaten

Preheat pizzelle iron according to manufacturer's directions. Mix flour, sugar, margarine, anise extract and eggs. Drop 1 tablespoon batter onto heated pizzelle iron; close. Cook about 30 seconds or until golden brown. Carefully remove pizzelle from iron. Cool on wire rack. Repeat for each cookie. **about 3½ dozen cookies**

PER SERVING: Calories 80; Protein 1 g; Carbohydrate 10 g; Fat 4 g; Cholesterol 20 mg; Sodium 45 mg

Krumkake

Making these charming cookies takes a little practice. Be prepared to adjust the heat and cooking time to get the desired color. Each hot cookie wafer is quickly rolled around a cone-shaped mold. Using two molds is easier; if only one is available, remove it from the cooling cookie before the next cookie is done. Try serving krumkakes filled with whipped cream, lightly sweetened, or garnished with fruit.

1 cup sugar
¾ cup all-purpose flour
½ cup margarine or butter, melted
⅓ cup whipping (heavy) cream
2 teaspoons cornstarch
1 teaspoon vanilla
4 eggs

Beat all ingredients until smooth. Heat krumkake iron over small electric or gas unit on medium-high heat until hot (grease iron lightly if necessary). Pour scant tablespoon batter on iron; close gently. Heat each side about 15 seconds or until light golden brown. Keep iron over heat at all times. Carefully remove cookie. Immediately roll around cone-shaped roller. Remove roller when cookie is set.

about 4 dozen cookies

PER SERVING: Calories 60; Protein 1 g; Carbohydrate 6 g; Fat 3 g; Cholesterol 20 mg; Sodium 30 mg

Cookie-Mold Cookies

Slightly spicy with a hint of almond, these cookies are reminiscent of the Dutch-inspired, store-bought cookies in the shape of windmills. If you have windmill molds, use them, but any cookie mold will do.

¾ **cup packed brown sugar**
½ **cup margarine or butter, softened**
¼ **cup molasses**
½ **teaspoon vanilla**
1 **egg**
2¼ **cups all-purpose flour**
¾ **cup coarsely chopped sliced almonds**
½ **teaspoon ground allspice**
¼ **teaspoon salt**
¼ **teaspoon baking soda**

Mix brown sugar, margarine, molasses, vanilla and egg in large bowl. Stir in remaining ingredients. Cover and refrigerate 2 hours or until firm.

Heat oven to 350°. Lightly grease cookie sheet. Flour wooden or ceramic cookie mold(s). Tap mold to remove excess flour. Firmly press small amounts of dough into mold, adding more dough until mold is full and making sure dough is of uniform thickness across mold. Hold mold upside down and tap edge firmly several times on hard surface (such as a counter or cutting board). If cookie does not come out, turn mold and tap another edge until cookie comes out of mold. Place cookies on cookie sheet. Bake 8 to 10 minutes for 2-inch cookies, 10 to 12 minutes for 5-inch cookies or until edges are light brown. (Time depends on thickness of cookies. Watch carefully.)

**about 4½ dozen 2-inch cookies
or 2 dozen 5-inch cookies**

PER SERVING: Calories 60; Protein 1 g; Carbohydrate 8 g; Fat 3 g; Cholesterol 5 mg; Sodium 35 mg

Decorating Cookies

Below you'll find fun cookie decorating ideas:

• Sprinkle frosted or iced cookies with chopped nuts. Press the nuts into the topping while it is still wet; that way, the nuts will hold fast to the cookie.

• Arrange raisins, currants or candied cherry halves or cherry cutouts on pale-frosted cookies before the frosting or icing sets.

• Press cinnamon candies into cookie-dough cutouts before baking. Although the candies soften with heating, they don't melt enough to spread. The design you make with the candies will be unchanged when the cookies come out of the oven.

• Christmas cookies just wouldn't be the same without red- and green-colored sugars. Dust unbaked cookies with sugar or sprinkle it over frosted or iced cookies.

• Jimmies, sprinkles and chocolate shots are colorful ways to decorate unbaked or frosted cookies without any fuss—just sprinkle!

• Turn rolled cookies into hanging ornaments. Use a drinking straw to poke a hole in the dough at the top of the cookie before baking. When the baked cookie has cooled, slip a length of yarn through the hole.

Coconut Macaroons

3 egg whites
¼ teaspoon cream of tartar
⅛ teaspoon salt
¾ cup sugar
¼ teaspoon almond extract
2 cups flaked coconut
12 candied cherries, each cut into
    fourths

Heat oven to 300°. Grease cookie sheet lightly. Beat egg whites, cream of tartar and salt in medium bowl until foamy. Beat in sugar, 1 tablespoon at a time. Continue beating until stiff and glossy. Do not underbeat. Fold in almond extract and coconut.

Drop mixture by teaspoonfuls about 1 inch apart onto cookie sheet. Place a cherry piece on each cookie. Bake 20 to 25 minutes or just until edges are light brown. Cool 10 minutes; remove from cookie sheet.   **3½ to 4 dozen cookies**

MINT MACAROONS: Substitute ¼ teaspoon peppermint extract for the almond extract. After beating, fold in 1 package (6 ounces) semisweet chocolate chips (1 cup), reserving 3½ to 4 dozen chocolate chips. Substitute reserved chips for the cherry pieces.

PER SERVING: Calories 40; Protein 0 g; Carbohydrate 6 g; Fat 2 g; Cholesterol 0 mg; Sodium 30 mg

Brown Sugar Drops

2 cups packed brown sugar
½ cup shortening
½ cup margarine or butter, softened
½ cup milk
2 eggs
3½ cups all-purpose flour
1 teaspoon baking soda
½ teaspoon salt
Butter Frosting (below)

Heat oven to 400°. Mix brown sugar, shortening, margarine, milk and eggs in large bowl. Stir in remaining ingredients except Butter Frosting.

Drop dough by rounded tablespoonfuls about 2 inches apart onto ungreased cookie sheet. Bake 9 to 11 minutes or until almost no indentation remains when touched in center. Cool slightly; remove from cookie sheet. Cool completely. Prepare Butter Frosting and spread on cookies.   **about 5 dozen cookies**

Butter Frosting

4 cups powdered sugar
½ cup margarine or butter, melted
2 teaspoons vanilla
2 to 4 tablespoons milk

Beat all ingredients until smooth and of spreading consistency.

APPLESAUCE-BROWN SUGAR DROPS: Substitute 1 cup applesauce for the milk. Stir in 1½ teaspoons ground cinnamon, ¼ teaspoon ground cloves and 1 cup raisins.

about 5 dozen cookies

PER SERVING: Calories 130; Protein 1 g; Carbohydrate 21 g; Fat 5 g; Cholesterol 5 mg; Sodium 75 mg

Candy Cookies

A pleasing variation on the classic choco-late chip cookie—have fun selecting the type of candy you use.

½ cup granulated sugar
½ cup packed brown sugar
⅓ cup margarine or butter, softened
⅓ cup shortening
1 teaspoon vanilla
1 egg
1½ cups all-purpose flour
½ teaspoon baking soda
½ teaspoon salt
1 package (8 ounces) chocolate-coated candies

Heat oven to 375°. Mix sugars, margarine, short-ening, vanilla and egg. Stir in remaining ingredi-ents. Drop dough by heaping teaspoonfuls about 2 inches apart onto ungreased cookie sheet. Bake until light brown, 8 to 10 minutes. (Centers will be soft.) Cool slightly; remove from cookie sheet. **about 3 dozen cookies**

PER SERVING: Calories 100; Protein 1 g; Carbohy-drate 15 g; Fat 4 g; Cholesterol 5 mg; Sodium 65 mg

Soft Pumpkin Drops

1 cup sugar
1 cup canned pumpkin
½ cup shortening
1 tablespoon grated orange peel
2 cups all-purpose or whole wheat flour
1 teaspoon baking powder
1 teaspoon baking soda
1 teaspoon ground cinnamon
¼ teaspoon salt
½ cup raisins
½ cup chopped nuts
Creamy Vanilla Frosting (below)

Heat oven to 375°. Mix sugar, pumpkin, shorten-ing and orange peel. Stir in flour, baking powder, baking soda, cinnamon and salt. Mix in raisins and nuts. Drop by rounded teaspoonfuls about 2 inches apart onto ungreased cookie sheet. Bake until light brown, 8 to 10 minutes; cool. Frost with Creamy Vanilla Frosting.

about 4 dozen cookies

CHOCOLATE CHIP-PUMPKIN DROPS: Substitute semisweet chocolate chips for the raisins or nuts.

Creamy Vanilla Frosting

3 cups powdered sugar
⅓ cup margarine or butter, softened
1½ teaspoons vanilla
About 2 tablespoons milk

Mix powdered sugar and margarine. Stir in va-nilla and milk; beat until smooth and of spread-ing consistency.

PER SERVING: Calories; 110; Protein 1 g; Carbohy-drate 18 g; Fat 4 g; Cholesterol 0 mg; Sodium 60 mg

Chocolate Chip Cookies

Chocolate Chip Cookies

You'll find these traditional favorites are always a hit—at parties, for drop-in guests, or for dessert any time!

¾ **cup granulated sugar**
¾ **cup packed brown sugar**
1 **cup margarine or butter, softened**
1 **egg**
2¼ **cups all-purpose or whole wheat
    flour**
1 **teaspoon baking soda**
½ **teaspoon salt**
1 **cup coarsely chopped nuts**
1 **package (12 ounces) semisweet choco-
    late chips (2 cups)**

Heat oven to 375°. Mix sugars, margarine and egg in large bowl. Stir in flour, baking soda and salt. (Dough will be stiff.) Stir in nuts and chocolate chips.

Drop dough by rounded tablespoonfuls about 2 inches apart onto ungreased cookie sheet. Bake 8 to 10 minutes or until light brown. (Centers will be soft.) Cool slightly; remove from cookie sheet.   **about 4 dozen cookies**

PER SERVING: Calories 140; Protein 1 g; Carbohydrate 16 g; Fat 8 g; Cholesterol 5 mg; Sodium 90 mg

Chocolate Crinkles

2 **cups granulated sugar**
½ **cup vegetable oil**
4 **ounces unsweetened chocolate, melted
    and cooled**
2 **teaspoons vanilla**
4 **eggs**
2 **cups all-purpose flour**
2 **teaspoons baking powder**
½ **teaspoon salt**
1 **cup powdered sugar**

Mix granulated sugar, oil, chocolate and vanilla. Mix in eggs, 1 at a time. Stir in flour, baking powder and salt. Cover and refrigerate at least 3 hours.

Heat oven to 350°. Drop dough by teaspoonfuls into powdered sugar; roll around to coat. Shape into balls. Place about 2 inches apart on greased cookie sheet. Bake until almost no indentation remains when touched, 10 to 12 minutes.   **about 6 dozen cookies**

PER SERVING: Calories 70; Protein 1 g; Carbohydrate 10 g; Fat 3 g; Cholesterol 10 mg; Sodium 30 mg

Brownies, Milk Chocolate-Malt Brownies (page 25)

2

Best Brownies and Bars

Brownies

Brownies are a welcome addition any time during the holidays—plus they are great for mailing.

5 squares (1 ounce each) unsweetened chocolate
⅔ cup margarine or butter
1¾ cups sugar
2 teaspoons vanilla
3 eggs
1 cup all-purpose flour
1 cup chopped nuts
1 package (6 ounces) semisweet chocolate chips (1 cup), if desired
Chocolate Frosting (right)

Heat oven to 350°. Grease square pan, 9 × 9 × 2 inches. Heat chocolate and margarine over low heat, stirring frequently, until melted; remove from heat. Cool slightly. Beat sugar, vanilla and eggs in large bowl on high speed 5 minutes. Beat in chocolate mixture on low speed. Beat in flour just until blended. Stir in nuts and chocolate chips.

Spread batter in pan. Bake 40 to 45 minutes or just until brownies begin to pull away from sides of pan. Cool completely. Spread with Chocolate Frosting. **24 brownies**

Chocolate Frosting

2 ounces unsweetened chocolate
2 tablespoons margarine or butter
2 cups powdered sugar
3 tablespoons hot water

Heat chocolate and margarine in 2-quart saucepan over low heat until melted; remove from heat. Stir in powdered sugar and water until smooth. (If frosting is too thick, add more water. If frosting is too thin, add more powdered sugar.)

PER SERVING: Calories 240; Protein 3 g; Carbohydrate 26 g; Fat 14 g; Cholesterol 25 mg; Sodium 70 mg

Tips for Bar Cookies

Use the pan size called for in the recipe. If you don't have the correct pan, choose a different type of cookie. Make sure that the cookie dough is spread to the sides and right into the corners of the pan. If you are not sure when the cookies are done, insert a wooden pick into the center of the pan. If it comes out wet, they need more time. Let bar cookies cool completely in the pan unless the recipe directs otherwise.

Marbled Brownies

Cream Cheese Filling (below)
1 cup margarine or butter
**4 squares (1 ounce each) unsweetened
    chocolate**
2 cups sugar
2 teaspoons vanilla
4 eggs
1½ cups all-purpose flour
½ teaspoon salt
1 cup coarsely chopped nuts

Heat oven to 350°. Prepare Cream Cheese Filling. Heat margarine and chocolate over low heat, stirring occasionally, until melted; cool. Beat chocolate mixture, sugar, vanilla and eggs in 2½-quart bowl on medium speed, scraping bowl occasionally, 1 minute. Beat in flour and salt on low speed, scraping bowl occasionally, 30 seconds. Beat on medium speed 1 minutes. Stir in nuts.

Spread half of the batter in greased square pan, 9 × 9 × 2 inches; spread with Cream Cheese Filling. Gently spread remaining batter over Cream Cheese Filling. Gently swirl through batter with spoon in an over-and-under motion for marbled effect. Bake until wooden pick inserted in center comes out clean, 55 to 65 minutes; cool. Cut into bars, about 1½ × 1 inch.

48 bars

Cream Cheese Filling

¼ cup sugar
1 teaspoon ground cinnamon
1½ teaspoons vanilla
1 egg
**1 package (8 ounces) cream cheese,
    softened**

Beat all ingredients in 1½-quart bowl, scraping bowl occasionally, 2 minutes.

PER SERVING: Calories 145; Protein 2 g; Carbohydrate 14 g; Fat 9 g; Cholesterol 25 mg; Sodium 90 mg

Fruit-filled Brownies

Use your favorite flavor of preserves or spreadable fruit to personalize these brownies.

⅔ cup shortening
**4 squares (1 ounce each) unsweetened
    chocolate**
2 cups sugar
4 eggs
1½ cups all-purpose flour
1 teaspoon baking powder
1 teaspoon salt
**Apricot or peach preserves or orange
    marmalade**
Quick Chocolate Frosting (below)

Heat oven to 350°. Line jelly roll pan, 15½ × 10½ × 1 inch, with aluminum foil; grease. Heat shortening and chocolate in 3-quart saucepan over low heat, stirring constantly, until melted. Remove from heat; beat in sugar and eggs until smooth. Stir in flour, baking powder and salt. Spread in pan. Bake until slight indentation remains when touched, about 20 minutes; cool.

Remove brownies from pan; remove aluminum foil. Cut ¼-inch strip from each long side of brownies; cut ¾-inch strip from each end. Discard strips. Cut remaining piece crosswise into halves. Spread 1 half with preserves; top with remaining half. Spread top with Quick Chocolate Frosting. Cut into bars, about 2 × 1 inch.

35 brownies

Quick Chocolate Frosting

Heat 1 bar (4 ounces) sweet cooking chocolate over low heat, stirring constantly, until melted.

PER SERVING: Calories 150; Protein 2 g; Carbohydrate 20 g; Fat 7 g; Cholesterol 25 mg; Sodium 80 mg

Milk Chocolate-Malt Brownies

This luscious brownie is almost a candy confection.

1 package (11.5 ounces) milk chocolate chips (2 cups)
½ cup margarine or butter
¾ cup sugar
1 teaspoon vanilla
3 eggs
1¾ cups all-purpose flour
½ cup instant malted milk
½ teaspoon baking powder
¼ teaspoon salt
1 cup malted milk balls, coarsely chopped

Heat oven to 350°. Grease rectangular pan, 13 × 9 × 2 inches. Heat milk chocolate and margarine in 3-quart saucepan over low heat, stirring frequently, until melted; remove from heat. Cool slightly. Beat in sugar, vanilla and eggs. Stir in remaining ingredients except malted milk balls.

Spread batter in pan. Sprinkle with malted milk balls. Bake 30 to 35 minutes or until toothpick inserted in center comes out clean. Cool completely. **48 brownies**

PER SERVING: Calories 90; Protein 1 g; Carbohydrate 12 g; Fat 4 g; Cholesterol 15 mg; Sodium 50 mg

Amaretto Brownies

For the sophisticated brownie lover!

⅔ cup blanched almonds, toasted
8 ounces semisweet chocolate
⅓ cup margarine or butter
1¼ cups all-purpose flour
1 cup sugar
2 tablespoons amaretto or 1 teaspoon almond extract
1 teaspoon baking powder
½ teaspoon salt
2 eggs
Amaretto Frosting (below)

Heat oven to 350°. Grease rectangular pan, 13 × 9 × 2 inches. Place ⅓ cup almonds in food processor. Cover and process, using quick on-and-off motions, until almonds are ground. Chop remaining almonds; reserve. Heat chocolate and margarine in 3-quart saucepan over low heat, stirring frequently, until melted; remove from heat. Stir in ground almonds and remaining ingredients except Amaretto Frosting and chopped almonds.

Spread batter in pan. Bake 22 to 27 minutes or until toothpick inserted in center comes out clean. Cool completely. Prepare Amaretto Frosting and spread on brownies; sprinkle with reserved chopped almonds. **32 brownies**

Amaretto Frosting

2 cups powdered sugar
3 tablespoons margarine or butter, softened
1 tablespoon amaretto or ¼ teaspoon almond extract
1 to 2 tablespoons milk

Mix all ingredients until smooth.

PER SERVING: Calories 165; protein 2 g; Carbohydrate 23 g; Fat 7 g; Cholesterol 15 mg; Sodium 85 mg

Mousse Brownies

½ cup margarine or butter
1 package (12 ounces) semisweet chocolate chips (2 cups)
1⅔ cups sugar
1¼ cups all-purpose flour
1 teaspoon vanilla
½ teaspoon baking powder
½ teaspoon salt
3 eggs
1 cup chopped nuts
Mousse Topping (below)

Heat oven to 350°. Grease rectangular pan, 13 × 9 × 2 inches. Heat margarine and chocolate chips in 3-quart saucepan over low heat, stirring constantly, until melted. Stir in remaining ingredients except nuts and Mousse Topping until smooth; stir in nuts, if desired. Spread in pan.

Prepare Mousse Topping; pour evenly over batter. Bake 45 minutes; cool 2 hours. Cut into 1½- or 2-inch squares.   **48 or 24 brownies**

Mousse Topping

¾ cup whipping (heavy) cream
1 package (6 ounces) semisweet chocolate chips (1 cup)
3 eggs
⅓ cup sugar
⅛ teaspoon salt

Heat whipping cream and chocolate chips in 2-quart saucepan, stirring constantly, until chocolate is melted and mixture is smooth; cool slightly. Beat remaining ingredients until foamy; stir into chocolate mixture.

PER SERVING: Calories 150; Protein 2 g; Carbohydrate 18 g; Fat 8 g; Cholesterol 30 mg; Sodium 55 mg

Cocoa Brownies

This is the one for all those people who like cakelike, tender brownies.

1 cup sugar
½ cup shortening
1 teaspoon vanilla
2 eggs
⅔ cup all-purpose flour
½ cup cocoa
½ teaspoon baking powder
¼ teaspoon salt
½ cup chopped walnuts, if desired

Heat oven to 350°. Grease square pan, 9 × 9 × 2 inches. Mix sugar, shortening, vanilla and eggs in large bowl. Stir in remaining ingredients except nuts. Stir in nuts.

Spread batter in pan. Bake 20 to 25 minutes or until toothpick inserted in center comes out clean. Cool completely.   **16 brownies**

TURTLE BROWNIES: Omit walnuts. Sprinkle ½ cup coarsely chopped pecans over batter before baking. Bake as directed. Heat 12 vanilla caramels and 1 tablespoon milk over low heat, stirring frequently, until caramels are melted. Drizzle over warm brownies. Cool completely.

PER SERVING: Calories 170; Protein 2 g; Carbohydrate 19 g; Fat 10 g; Cholesterol 25 mg; Sodium 55 mg

Turtle Brownies

Peanut Butter Swirl Brownies

The "hills" created when the knife is drawn through the batter to make a swirl effect level off while the brownies bake.

⅔ **cup granulated sugar**
½ **cup packed brown sugar**
½ **cup margarine or butter, softened**
2 **tablespoons milk**
2 **eggs**
¾ **cup all-purpose flour**
½ **teaspoon baking powder**
¼ **teaspoon salt**
¼ **cup peanut butter**
⅓ **cup peanut butter–flavored chips**
⅓ **cup cocoa**
⅓ **cup semisweet chocolate chips**

Heat oven to 350°. Grease square pan, 9 × 9 × 2 inches. Mix sugars, margarine, milk and eggs in large bowl. Stir in flour, baking powder and salt. Divide batter in half (about 1 cup plus 2 tablespoons for each half). Stir peanut butter and peanut butter chips into one half. Stir cocoa and chocolate chips into remaining half.

Spoon chocolate batter into pan in 8 mounds, checkerboard style. Spoon peanut butter batter between mounds of chocolate batter. Gently swirl knife through batter for marbled effect. Bake 30 to 35 minutes or until toothpick inserted in center comes out clean. Cool completely. **16 brownies**

PER SERVING: Calories 220; Protein 4 g; Carbohydrate 26 g; Fat 11 g; Cholesterol 25 mg; Sodium 160 mg

Toffee Bars

1 **cup packed brown sugar**
1 **cup margarine or butter, softened**
1 **teaspoon vanilla**
1 **egg yolk**
2 **cups all-purpose flour**
¼ **teaspoon salt**
1 **bar (4 ounces) milk chocolate candy**
½ **cup chopped nuts**

Heat oven to 350°. Mix brown sugar, margarine, vanilla and egg yolk. Stir in flour and salt. Press in greased rectangular pan, 13 × 9 × 2 inches.

Bake until very light brown, 25 to 30 minutes (crust will be soft). Immediately place separated pieces of chocolate candy on crust. Let stand until soft; spread evenly. Sprinkle with nuts. Cut into bars, about 2 × 1½ inches, while warm. **32 bars**

PER SERVING: Calories 140; Protein 1 g; Carbohydrate 15 g; Fat 8 g; Cholesterol 5 mg; Sodium 90 mg

Unbelievable Brownies

For brownies you can't wait to sink your teeth into, try these simple tricks.

1. Use a shiny metal or glass pan. Nonstick-coated pans cause brownies to be soggy and low in volume.

2. Line your pan with aluminum foil when making brownies. The cooled brownies lift right out, are easily cut into uniform squares, and there's no pan to wash!

3. To prevent crumbling, cut brownies when completely cool unless the recipe specifies otherwise.

4. Cut thoroughly cooled brownies with a plastic knife or table knife for smooth-sided bars.

Pumpkin Spice Bars

A fun—and easy—twist on pumpkin pie!

4 eggs
2 cups sugar
1 cup vegetable oil
1 can (16 ounces) pumpkin
2 cups all-purpose flour
2 teaspoons baking powder
2 teaspoons ground cinnamon
1 teaspoon baking soda
½ teaspoon salt
½ teaspoon ground ginger
¼ teaspoon ground cloves
1 cup raisins
Cream Cheese Frosting (below)
½ cup chopped nuts

Heat oven to 350°. Grease jelly roll pan, 15½ × 10½ × 1 inch. Beat eggs, sugar, oil and pumpkin in large bowl. Stir in flour, baking powder, cinnamon, baking soda, salt, ginger and cloves. Stir in raisins.

Pour batter into pan. Bake 25 to 30 minutes or until toothpick inserted in center comes out clean. Cool completely. Prepare Cream Cheese Frosting and spread on bars; sprinkle with nuts. **48 bars**

Cream Cheese Frosting

1 package (3 ounces) cream cheese, softened
⅓ cup margarine or butter, softened
1 teaspoon vanilla
2 cups powdered sugar

Beat cream cheese, margarine and vanilla in medium bowl on low speed until smooth. Gradually beat in powdered sugar until smooth.

PER SERVING: Calories 120; Protein 1 g; Carbohydrate 16 g; Fat 6 g; Cholesterol 20 mg; Sodium 75 mg

Caramel Candy Bars

1 package (14 ounces) vanilla caramels
⅓ cup milk
2 cups all-purpose flour
2 cups quick-cooking or regular oats
1½ cups packed brown sugar
1 teaspoon baking soda
½ teaspoon salt
1 egg
1 cup margarine or butter, softened
1 package (6 ounces) semisweet chocolate chips (1 cup)
1 cup chopped walnuts or dry roasted peanuts

Heat oven to 350°. Heat caramels and milk in 2-quart saucepan over low heat, stirring frequently, until smooth; remove from heat and reserve. Mix flour, oats, brown sugar, baking soda and salt in large bowl. Stir in egg and margarine with fork until mixture is crumbly.

Press half of the crumbly mixture in ungreased rectangular pan, 13 × 9 × 2 inches. Bake 10 minutes. Sprinkle with chocolate chips and walnuts. Drizzle with caramel mixture. Sprinkle remaining crumbly mixture over top. Bake 20 to 25 minutes or until golden brown. Cool 30 minutes. Loosen edges from sides of pan. Cool completely. **48 bars**

PER SERVING: Calories 160; Protein 2 g; Carbohydrate 22 g; Fat 7 g; Cholesterol 5 mg; Sodium 110 mg

Pecan Pie Squares

Pecan Pie Squares

3 cups all-purpose flour
⅓ cup sugar
¾ cup margarine or butter, softened
½ teaspoon salt
Filling (below)

Heat oven to 350°. Grease jelly roll pan, 15½ × 10½ × 1 inch. Beat flour, sugar, margarine and salt in large bowl on low speed until crumbly. (Mixture will be dry.) Press firmly in pan. Bake about 20 minutes or until light golden brown.

Prepare Filling and pour over baked layer; spread evenly. Bake about 25 minutes or until filling is set. Cool completely.   **60 squares**

Filling

1½ cups sugar
1½ cups corn syrup
3 tablespoons margarine or butter, melted
1½ teaspoons vanilla
4 eggs, slightly beaten
2½ cups chopped pecans

Mix all ingredients except pecans in large bowl until well blended. Stir in pecans.

PER SERVING: Calories 140; Protein 1 g; Carbohydrate 18 g; Fat 7 g; Cholesterol 15 mg; Sodium 65 mg

Lemon Squares

1 cup all-purpose flour
½ cup margarine or butter, softened
¼ cup powdered sugar
1 cup granulated sugar
2 tablespoons lemon juice
2 teaspoons grated lemon peel, if desired
½ teaspoon baking powder
¼ teaspoon salt
2 eggs

Heat oven to 350°. Mix flour, margarine and powdered sugar. Press in ungreased square pan, 8 × 8 × 2 or 9 × 9 × 2 inches, building up ½-inch edges. Bake 20 minutes. Beat remaining ingredients about 3 minutes or until light and fluffy. Pour over hot crust.

Bake about 25 minutes or until no indentation remains when touched lightly in center; cool. Sprinkle with powdered sugar if desired. Cut into 1½-inch squares.   **25 squares**

LEMON-COCONUT SQUARES: Stir ½ cup flaked coconut into egg mixture.

PER SERVING: Calories 90; Protein 1 g; Carbohydrate 13 g; Fat 4 g; Cholesterol 22 mg; Sodium 80 mg

Coconut Cheesecake Bars

1 cup graham cracker crumbs (about 12 squares)
¼ cup finely chopped pecans
3 tablespoons margarine or butter, melted
1 package (8 ounces) cream cheese, softened
½ cup sugar
¼ cup milk
½ cup shredded or flaked coconut, toasted
1 teaspoon vanilla
3 eggs

Heat oven to 325°. Mix cracker crumbs, pecans and margarine thoroughly. Press evenly in bottom of ungreased rectangular baking dish, 11 × 7 × 1½ inches. Bake about 10 minutes or until set.

Beat cream cheese until creamy. Beat in sugar, milk, coconut and vanilla. Beat in eggs, one at a time. Spread mixture over crust. Bake about 30 minutes or until center is set. Cover and refrigerate at least 2 hours. Cut into 2¼ × 1¼-inch bars. Place a pecan half on each bar if desired. Refrigerate any remaining bars.

25 bars

TO MICROWAVE: Prepare crust as directed—except press crumb mixture evenly in rectangular microwavable dish, 11 × 7 × 1½ inches. Elevate dish on inverted microwavable dinner plate in microwave oven. Microwave uncovered on medium (50%) 4 to 6 minutes, rotating dish ¼ turn after 2 minutes, until mixture appears dry.

Prepare filling and spread over crust as directed. Microwave (do not elevate) uncovered 14 to 19 minutes, rotating dish ¼ turn every 3 minutes, until filling is set. Continue as directed.

PER SERVING: Calories 100; Protein 2 g; Carbohydrate 8 g; Fat 7 g; Cholesterol 45 mg; Sodium 80 mg

Cream-filled Oat Bars

Wonderfully creamy in the center, these golden brown bars are an exceptional treat.

1 can (14 ounces) sweetened condensed milk
2 teaspoons grated lemon peel
¼ cup lemon juice
1¼ cups all-purpose flour
1 cup quick-cooking or regular oats
½ cup packed brown sugar
½ cup margarine or butter, softened
¼ teaspoon salt
¼ teaspoon baking soda

Heat oven to 375°. Grease square pan, 9 × 9 × 2 inches. Mix milk, lemon peel and lemon juice until thickened; reserve. Mix remaining ingredients until crumbly.

Press half of the crumbly mixture in pan. Bake about 10 minutes or until set. Spread milk mixture over baked layer. Sprinkle remaining crumbly mixture on milk mixture. Press gently into milk mixture. Bake about 20 minutes or until edge is golden brown and center is set but soft. Cool completely.

24 bars

PER SERVING: Calories 150; Protein 2 g; Carbohydrate 21 g; Fat 6 g; Cholesterol 5 mg; Sodium 100 mg

Cream-filled Oat Bars, Caramel Candy Bars (page 29)

Chocolate Nesselrode Cake

3
Glorious Cakes and Pies

Chocolate Nesselrode Cake

Nesselrode was originally a pudding created by the chef to a 19th-century Russian count of the same name. Today a brandy- or rum-flavored mixture of candied fruits, chestnuts and raisins is often served as a dessert sauce.

> 2 cups all-purpose flour
> 2 cups sugar
> ¾ cup water
> ¾ cup buttermilk
> ½ cup shortening
> 1 teaspoon baking soda
> 1 teaspoon salt
> 1 teaspoon vanilla
> ½ teaspoon baking powder
> 2 eggs
> 4 ounces melted unsweetened chocolate (cool)
> Nesselrode Filling (right)
> Cocoa Fluff (right)

Heat oven to 350°. Grease and flour three 8-inch round layer pans. Beat all ingredients except Nesselrode Filling and Cocoa Fluff in large mixer bowl on low speed, scraping bowl constantly, 30 seconds. Beat on high speed, scraping bowl occasionally, 3 minutes. Pour into pans. Bake until wooden pick inserted in center comes out clean, 30 to 35 minutes. Cool. Fill layers and frost top of cake with Nesselrode Filling. Frost side of cake with Cocoa Fluff. Refrigerate. **16 servings**

Nesselrode Filling

> 1 cup heavy whipping cream
> ¼ cup powdered sugar
> ¼ cup Nesselrode*

Beat whipping cream and powdered sugar in chilled bowl until stiff. Fold in Nesselrode.

*¼ cup finely cut-up candied fruit and 1 teaspoon rum flavoring can be substituted for the Nesselrode.

Cocoa Fluff

> 1 cup heavy whipping cream
> ¼ cup powdered sugar
> 2 tablespoons cocoa

Beat all ingredients together in chilled bowl until stiff.

NOTE: Cake can be baked in two 9-inch round layer pans. When cool, split to make 4 layers. Fill layers and frost top of cake with one-quarter each of the Nesselrode Filling.

PER SERVING: Calories 395; Protein 4 g; Carbohydrate 47 g; Fat 21 g; Cholesterol 60 mg; Sodium 240 mg

Decadent Chocolate Cake with Raspberry Sauce

1 cup semisweet chocolate chips
½ cup margarine or butter
½ cup all-purpose flour or cake flour
4 eggs, separated
½ cup sugar
½ cup semisweet chocolate chips
2 tablespoons margarine or butter
2 tablespoons corn syrup
Raspberry Sauce (right)

Heat oven to 325°. Grease springform pan, 8 × 2½ inches, or round pan, 9 × 1½ inches. Heat 1 cup chocolate chips and ½ cup margarine in 2-quart heavy saucepan over medium heat until chocolate chips are melted; cool 5 minutes. Stir in flour until smooth. Stir in egg yolks until well blended.

Beat egg whites in large bowl on high speed until foamy. Beat in sugar, 1 tablespoon at a time, until soft peaks form. Fold chocolate mixture into egg whites. Spread in pan.

Bake springform 35 to 40 minutes, round 30 to 35 minutes (top will appear dry and cracked) or until wooden pick inserted in center comes out clean; cool 10 minutes. Run knife along side of cake to loosen; remove side of springform pan. Invert cake onto wire rack; remove bottom of springform pan and cool cake completely. Place on serving plate.

Heat ½ cup chocolate chips, 2 tablespoons margarine and the corn syrup over medium heat until chocolate chips are melted. Spread over top of cake, allowing some to drizzle down side. Serve with Raspberry Sauce. Garnish with fresh raspberries and sweetened whipped cream if desired. **12 servings**

Raspberry Sauce

1 package (10 ounces) frozen raspberries, thawed, drained and juice reserved
¼ cup sugar
2 tablespoons cornstarch
1 to 2 tablespoons orange- or raspberry-flavored liqueur, if desired

Add enough water to reserved juice to measure 1 cup. Mix sugar and cornstarch in 1-quart saucepan. Stir in juice and raspberries. Heat to boiling over medium heat. Boil and stir 1 minute; strain. Stir in liqueur.

PER SERVING: Calories 325; Protein 4 g; Carbohydrate 39 g; Fat 18 g; Cholesterol 90 mg; Sodium 140

Storing Cakes

- Unfrosted cakes should be cooled completely before storing. They will become sticky if covered while warm.
- Foam-type cakes will stay fresh overnight stored in their baking pan and covered with waxed paper. Remove from pan and frost the day they are served.
- Cakes with creamy-type frosting can be stored in a cake safe or under a large inverted bowl. They can also be loosely covered with aluminum foil, plastic wrap or waxed paper.
- Cakes with fluffy frosting should be served the same day they are made. If it is necessary to store this type of cake, use a cake safe or inverted bowl, with a knife slipped under the edge, so the container is not airtight.
- Cakes with whipped cream toppings, cream fillings or cream cheese frostings should be refrigerated.

Raspberry-White Chocolate Cream Cake

Raspberry Filling (below)
3 ounces white baking bar, chopped
2¼ cups all-purpose flour
1½ cups sugar
2¼ teaspoons baking powder
½ teaspoon salt
1⅔ cups whipping (heavy) cream
3 eggs
1 teaspoon almond extract
White Chocolate Frosting (right)
White Chocolate Poinsettias, if desired
   (right)

Prepare Raspberry Filling. Heat oven to 350°. Grease and flour 2 round pans, 8 or 9 × 1½ inches. Heat white baking bar over low heat, stirring occasionally, until melted; cool. Mix flour, sugar, baking powder and salt; reserve. Beat whipping cream in chilled large bowl until stiff; reserve. Beat eggs about 5 minutes or until thick and lemon colored; beat in melted baking bar and almond extract.

Fold egg mixture into whipped cream. Add flour mixture, about ½ cup at a time, folding gently after each addition until blended. Pour into pans. Bake 8-inch rounds 35 to 40 minutes, 9-inch rounds 30 to 35 minutes or until toothpick inserted in center comes out clean. Cool 10 minutes; remove from pans. Cool completely on wire racks.

Fill layers with Raspberry Filling. Prepare White Chocolate Frosting; spread over side and top of cake. If adding poinsettias, reserve 1 tablespoon frosting.   **16 servings**

Raspberry Filling

¼ cup sugar
2 tablespoons cornstarch
⅛ teaspoon salt

1 cup raspberry-flavored wine cooler or
   sparkling raspberry juice
1 tablespoon margarine or butter
⅛ teaspoon almond extract
2 or 3 drops red food color, if desired

Mix sugar, cornstarch and salt in 1½-quart saucepan. Stir in wine cooler. Cook over medium heat, stirring constantly, until mixture thickens and boils. Boil and stir 1 minute; remove from heat. Stir in remaining ingredients. Cover and refrigerate until chilled.

White Chocolate Frosting

3 ounces white baking bar, chopped
3 cups powdered sugar
2 tablespoons plus 2 teaspoons raspberry-flavored wine cooler or water
2 tablespoons margarine or butter, softened
¼ teaspoon almond extract

Heat white baking bar over low heat, stirring occasionally, until melted; cool. Beat melted baking bar and remaining ingredients in medium bowl on medium speed until smooth and of spreading consistency. If necessary, stir in additional wine cooler, 1 teaspoon at a time.

White Chocolate Poinsettias

Heat vanilla-flavored candy-coating in small saucepan over low heat, stirring constantly, until melted. Stir in a tiny amount of red paste food color until desired shade is achieved. Paint coating mixture on back side of fresh mint leaves or washable artificial leaves that resemble poinsettia leaves; let dry. Peel coating from leaves; arrange on cake. Drop a spoonful of reserved frosting in the center of leaves; dot with red cake decorating gel.

PER SERVING: Calories 435; Protein 51 g; Carbohydrate 65 g; Fat 17 g; Cholesterol 65 mg; Sodium 190 mg

Best Chocolate Cake with Fudge Frosting

A chocolate treat that's a satisfying ending to any meal. For a quicker cake, try the sheet cake in the 13 × 9 × 2-inch pan.

2 cups all-purpose flour
2 cups sugar
½ cup shortening
¾ cup water
¾ cup buttermilk
1 teaspoon baking soda
1 teaspoon salt
1 teaspoon vanilla
½ teaspoon baking powder
2 eggs
4 ounces unsweetened chocolate, melted and cooled
Fudge Frosting (right)

Heat oven to 350°. Grease and flour rectangular pan, 13 × 9 × 2 inches, 3 round pans, 8 × 1½ inches, or 2 round pans, 9 × 1½ inches. Beat all ingredients except Fudge Frosting in large bowl on low speed 30 seconds, scraping bowl constantly. Beat on high speed 3 minutes, scraping bowl occasionally. Pour into pan(s).

Bake rectangular pan 40 to 45 minutes, round pans 30 to 35 minutes or until wooden pick inserted in center comes out clean. Cool rounds 10 minutes; remove from pans. Cool completely. Prepare Fudge Frosting; frost cake. (Fill layers with ⅓ cup frosting; frost side and top with remaining frosting.) **16 servings**

Fudge Frosting

2 cups sugar
½ cup shortening
⅔ cup milk
½ teaspoon salt
3 ounces unsweetened chocolate
2 teaspoons vanilla

Mix all ingredients except vanilla in 2½-quart saucepan. Heat to rolling boil, stirring occasionally. Boil 1 minute without stirring. Place saucepan in bowl of ice and water. Beat until frosting is smooth and of spreading consistency; stir in vanilla.

PER SERVING: Calories 450; Protein 4 g; Carbohydrate 67 g; Fat 21 g; Cholesterol 28 mg; Sodium 290 mg

Chocolate Curls

Place a bar of milk chocolate on waxed paper. Make chocolate curls by pulling a vegetable parer toward you, pressing firmly against the chocolate in long, thin strokes. Transfer each curl carefully with a wooden pick to waxed paper-lined cookie sheet or directly onto frosted cake, pie or dessert.

The curls will be easier to make if the chocolate is slightly warm. Let the chocolate stand in a warm place for about 15 minutes before making the curls. Semisweet chocolate can be used but the curls will be smaller. Thicker bars of chocolate will make larger curls.

Best Chocolate Cake with Fudge Frosting

Christmas Coconut Cake

2 cups all-purpose flour
1½ cups granulated sugar
3½ teaspoons baking powder
1 teaspoon salt
½ cup shortening
1 cup milk
1 teaspoon vanilla
4 egg whites
⅔ cup flaked coconut
Tutti-Frutti Filling (below)
1 cup whipping (heavy) cream
¼ cup powdered sugar
¾ teaspoon almond extract

Heat oven to 350°. Grease and flour 2 round layer pans, 9 × 1½ inches. Beat flour, granulated sugar, baking powder, salt, shortening, milk and vanilla in large mixer bowl on low speed, scraping bowl constantly, 30 seconds. Beat on high speed, scraping bowl occasionally, 2 minutes. Add egg whites; beat on high speed, scraping bowl occasionally, 2 minutes. Stir in coconut. Pour into pans.

Bake until wooden pick inserted in center comes out clean, 30 to 35 minutes; cool. Fill layers and frost top of cake to within 1 inch of edge with Tutti-Frutti Filling. Beat whipping cream, powdered sugar and almond extract in chilled bowl until stiff. Spread side and top edge of cake with whipped cream. Refrigerate.   **16 servings**

Tutti-Frutti Filling

2 egg yolks
⅔ cup sour cream
⅔ cup sugar
1 cup finely chopped pecans
⅔ cup flaked coconut
½ to 1 cup finely chopped raisins
½ to 1 cup finely chopped candied cherries

Mix egg yolks and sour cream in saucepan; stir in sugar. Cook over low heat, stirring constantly, until mixture begins to simmer. Simmer, stirring constantly, until mixture begins to thicken. Remove from heat; stir in remaining ingredients. Cool.

PER SERVING: Calories 430; Protein 5 g; Carbohydrate 55 g; Fat 21 g; Cholesterol 50 mg; Sodium 280 mg

Eggnog Pound Cake

1 cup sugar
½ cup butter or margarine, softened
2 tablespoons rum or 2 teaspoons rum flavoring
1 teaspoon vanilla
5 egg yolks
1¾ cups all-purpose flour
2 teaspoons baking powder
¾ teaspoon salt
½ teaspoon ground nutmeg
¾ cup milk

Heat oven to 350°. Grease and flour loaf pan, 9 × 5 × 3 inches. Beat sugar, butter, rum, vanilla and egg yolks in large bowl on low speed 30 seconds, scraping bowl constantly. Beat on high speed 5 minutes, scraping bowl occasionally. Beat in flour, baking powder, salt and nutmeg alternately with milk on low speed. Pour into pan.

Bake 50 to 60 minutes or until toothpick inserted in center comes out clean. Cool 10 minutes; remove from pan and cool completely.

                                16 servings

PER SERVING: Calories 180; Protein 2 g; Carbohydrate 24 g; Fat 8 g; Cholesterol 65 mg; Sodium 220 mg

Bûche de Noël

Bûche de Noël is French for "Christmas Log." If you wish, you can garnish this "log" with pine branches or mushrooms made out of meringue, available in gourmet food stores.

3 eggs
1 cup sugar
⅓ cup water
1 teaspoon vanilla
¾ cup all-purpose flour
1 teaspoon baking powder
¼ teaspoon salt
1 cup whipping (heavy) cream
2 tablespoons sugar
1½ teaspoons powdered instant coffee
Cocoa Frosting (right)

Heat oven to 375°. Line jelly roll pan, 15½ × 10½ × 1 inch, with aluminum foil or waxed paper; grease. Beat eggs in small mixer bowl on high speed until very thick and lemon colored, about 5 minutes. Pour eggs into large mixer bowl; gradually beat in 1 cup sugar. Beat in water and vanilla on low speed. Gradually add flour, baking powder and salt, beating just until batter is smooth. Pour into pan, spreading batter to corners. Bake until wooden pick inserted in center comes out clean, 12 to 15 minutes.

Loosen cake from edges of pan; immediately invert on towel generously sprinkled with powdered sugar. Remove foil; trim stiff edges of cake if necessary. While hot, roll cake and towel from narrow end. Cool on wire rack at least 30 minutes.

Beat whipping cream, 2 tablespoons sugar and the coffee in chilled bowl until stiff. Unroll cake; remove towel. Spread whipped cream mixture over cake. Roll up; frost with Cocoa Frosting. Make strokes with tines of fork to resemble bark. Decorate with Meringue Mushrooms. Store in refrigerator. **10 servings**

Cocoa Frosting

⅓ cup cocoa
⅓ cup margarine or butter, softened
2 cups powdered sugar
1½ teaspoons vanilla
1 to 2 tablespoons hot water

Mix cocoa and margarine. Stir in powdered sugar. Beat in vanilla and water until smooth and of spreading consistency.

PER SERVING: Calories 385; Protein 4 g; Carbohydrate 58 g; Fat 15 g; Cholesterol 90 mg; Sodium 190 mg

Reindeer Cake (page 44), Peppermint Bell Cake (page 45), Christmas Tree Cake

Christmas Tree Cake

Like to save a bit of time? Substitute your favorite cake and frosting mixes, instead of making the cake and frosting from scratch. This also works well for Reindeer Cake (page 44) and Peppermint Bell Cake (page 45).

Starlight Yellow Cake (page 44) or Best Chocolate Cake (page 38)
2 tablespoons green sugar
2 tablespoons multicolored nonpareils
White Mountain Frosting (below)

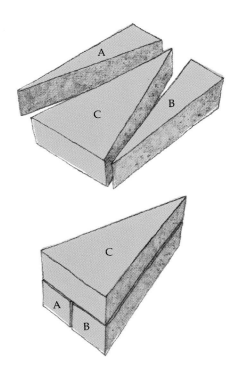

Heat oven to 350°. Grease and flour baking pan 13 × 9 × 2 inches. Prepare Starlight Yellow Cake or Best Chocolate Cake; pour into pan. Sprinkle batter with green sugar and nonpareils. Cut through batter with spatula to swirl. Bake as directed. Remove from pan; cool.

Cover large tray or piece of cardboard with aluminum foil or foil wrapping paper. Cut cake as shown in diagram. Prepare White Mountain Frosting. Tint with 1 or 2 drops green food color. Arrange cake pieces A and B on tray to make tree shape (see diagram); frost. Place piece C on top; frost sides and top, making strokes through frosting to resemble tree branches.

Sprinkle with green sugar. Decorate with cut-up gumdrops. Insert 3 peppermint candy sticks in end of cake to make trunk.   **16 servings**

White Mountain Frosting

½ cup sugar
¼ cup light corn syrup
2 tablespoons water
2 egg whites
1 teaspoon vanilla

Mix sugar, corn syrup and water in 1-quart saucepan. Cover and heat to rolling boil over medium heat. Uncover and cook, without stirring, to 242° on candy thermometer or until small amount of mixture dropped into very cold water forms a ball that flattens when removed from water. To get an accurate temperature reading it may be necessary to tilt the saucepan slightly. It takes 4 to 8 minutes for the syrup to reach 242°.

While mixture boils, beat egg whites in medium bowl just until stiff peaks form. Pour hot syrup very slowly in thin stream into egg whites, beating constantly on medium speed. Add vanilla. Beat on high speed about 10 minutes until stiff peaks form. Preparing this type of frosting on a humid day may require a longer beating time.

PER SERVING: Calories 520; Protein 4 g; Carbohydrate 97 g; Fat 13 g; Cholesterol 50 mg; Sodium 260 mg

Reindeer Cake

This cake is fun to decorate, especially for children! (See photo on page 42.)

Starlight Yellow Cake (below) or Best Chocolate Cake (page 38)
1 cup flaked coconut
White Mountain Frosting (page 43)

Bake Starlight Yellow Cake or Best Chocolate Cake in baking pan, 13 × 9 × 2 inches. Remove from pan and cool. Toast coconut in shallow baking pan in 350° oven, stirring frequently, until golden brown, about 5 minutes. Cut cake as shown in diagram. Arrange cake and pieces (ears) to form reindeer on aluminum foil-covered cardboard, 24 × 22 inches.

Prepare White Mountain Frosting. Frost sides and top of cake, joining pieces together. Sprinkle toasted coconut over reindeer. Use large chocolate wafers for eyes, red gumdrop for nose, red shoestring licorice for mouth and antlers.

16 servings

PER SERVING: Calories 525; Protein 4 g; Carbohydrate 94 g; Fat 15 g; Cholesterol 50 mg; Sodium 280 mg

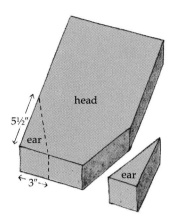

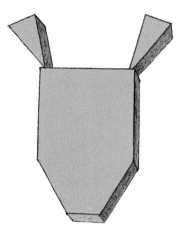

Starlight Yellow Cake

2¼ cups all-purpose flour
1½ cups sugar
½ cup shortening (half margarine or butter, softened, if desired)
1¼ cups milk
3½ teaspoons baking powder
1 teaspoon salt
1 teaspoon vanilla
3 eggs

Heat oven to 350°. Grease and flour rectangular pan, 13 × 9 × 2 inches, 2 round pans, 9 × 1½ inches or 3 round pans, 8 × 1½ inches. Beat all ingredients on low speed 30 seconds, scraping bowl constantly. Beat on high speed 3 minutes, scraping bowl occasionally. Pour into pan(s).

Bake rectangle 40 to 45 minutes, 9-inch rounds 30 to 35 minutes, 8-inch rounds 20 to 25 minutes or until wooden pick inserted in center comes out clean or until cake springs back when touched lightly in center. Cool rectangle on wire rack. Cool layers 10 minutes; remove from pans and cool completely on wire rack.

16 servings

PER SERVING: Calories 205; Protein 3 g; Carbohydrate 32 g; Fat 8 g; Cholesterol 55 mg; Sodium 280 mg

Peppermint Bell Cake

These holly gumdrops are also festive on other cakes or cupcakes.

Starlight Yellow Cake (page 44)
⅓ cup crushed peppermint candy
White Mountain Frosting (page 43)
½ to ¾ cup crushed peppermint candy
Gumdrop Holly (below)

Prepare Starlight Yellow Cake—except fold ⅓ cup crushed peppermint candy into batter. Bake in 2 round layer pans, 8 × 1½, or 3 round layer pans, 9 × 1½ inches. Fill and frost cake with White Mountain Frosting.

Coat side of cake with ½ to ¾ cup crushed peppermint candy, reserving 3 tablespoons for decoration. Draw outline of bells on top of cake or use cookie cutter. Outline bells using wooden pick dipped into red food color. Fill bells with reserved candy. Add Gumdrop Holly and red cinnamon candies.

Gumdrop Holly

Roll green gumdrops about ⅛ inch thick on heavily sugared board; cut to resemble holly leaves.

PER SERVING: Calories 530; Protein 4 g; Carbohydrate 99 g; Fat 13 g; Cholesterol 50 mg; Sodium 260 mg

Angel Food Cake Deluxe

Angel food cake is thought to have originated in St. Louis, Missouri, in the mid-19th century. Some people believe that the recipe was brought by slaves from the South up the Mississippi River to St. Louis. Others believe that angel food cake can be traced to the Pennsylvania Dutch.

1 cup cake flour
1½ cups powdered sugar
1½ cups egg whites (about 12)
1½ teaspoons cream of tartar
1 cup granulated sugar
1½ teaspoons vanilla
½ teaspoon almond extract
¼ teaspoon salt

Heat oven to 375°. Mix flour and powdered sugar. Beat egg whites and cream of tartar in large bowl on medium speed until foamy. Beat in granulated sugar on high speed, 2 tablespoons at a time, adding vanilla, almond extract and salt with the last addition of sugar; continue beating until meringue holds stiff peaks. Do not underbeat.

Sprinkle flour-sugar mixture, ¼ cup at a time, over meringue, folding in gently just until mixture disappears. Spread in ungreased tube pan, 10 × 4 inches. Gently cut through batter with spatula.

Bake 30 to 35 minutes or until cracks feel dry and top springs back when touched lightly. Immediately invert pan onto heatproof funnel; let hang until cake is completely cool.

16 servings

PER SERVING: Calories 130; Protein 3 g; Carbohydrate 50 g; Fat 0 g; Cholesterol 0 mg; Sodium 95 mg

Jeweled Fruitcake

This pretty cake gets its name from the large pieces of candied fruit and whole nuts that stud it throughout. If you like, wrap the fruitcake in cheesecloth; dampen with brandy, rum or wine; cover it tightly and refrigerate. Brush additional brandy on the cake every week, for as long as 2 months.

1 cup red and green maraschino cherries
¾ cup all-purpose flour
¾ cup sugar
½ teaspoon baking powder
½ teaspoon salt
1½ teaspoons vanilla
3 eggs
12 ounces Brazil nuts (about 1½ cups)
8 ounces dried apricots (about 2 cups)
8 ounces pitted dates (about 1½ cups)
5 ounces red and green candied pineapple, cut up (about 1 cup)

Heat oven to 300°. Line loaf pan, 9 × 5 × 3 or 8½ × 4½ × 2½ inches, with aluminum foil; grease. Mix all ingredients. Spread in pan.

Bake about 1 hour forty-five minutes or until wooden pick inserted in center comes out clean. If necessary, cover with aluminum foil last 30 minutes of baking to prevent excessive browning. Remove from pan; cool on wire rack. Wrap in plastic wrap; store in refrigerator.

32 servings

PER SERVING: Calories 155; Protein 2 g; Carbohydrate 25 g; Fat 6 g; Cholesterol 25 mg; Sodium 50 mg

Deep-Dish Cherry-Berry Pie

Pastry for 9-inch One-Crust Pie (page 47)
¾ cup sugar
½ cup all-purpose flour
2⅓ cups fresh red tart cherries, pitted*
2 cups fresh strawberries, cut in half**
1 teaspoon grated orange peel
1 tablespoon orange juice
Red food color, if desired
1 tablespoon butter or margarine

Heat oven to 425°. Generously grease square pan, 9 × 9 × 2 inches, or deep-dish pie plate, 9½ × 1¾ inches. Prepare pastry as directed—except roll into 10-inch square. Make cutouts near center so steam can escape. Mix sugar and flour in medium bowl; stir in cherries, strawberries, orange peel, orange juice and red food color. Turn into pan. Dot with butter. Fold pastry in half; place over fruit mixture. Fold edges of pastry just under inside edges of pan; press pastry to edges of pan. Bake about 55 minutes or until juice begins to bubble through cutouts in crust. Serve warm with whipping (heavy) cream if desired.

9 servings

PER SERVING: Calories 255; Protein 3 g; Carbohydrate 41 g; Fat 9 g; Cholesterol 10 mg; Sodium 130 mg

2 cans (about 16 ounces each) pitted red tart cherries, drained, can be substituted for the fresh cherries.

**2 cups frozen strawberries, thawed, drained and cut in half, can be substituted for the fresh strawberries.*

Favorite Pastry

One-Crust Pie; 9-inch

1 cup all-purpose flour
½ teaspoon salt
⅓ cup lard or ⅓ cup plus 1 tablespoon
   shortening
2 to 3 tablespoons cold water

One-Crust Pie; 10-inch

1⅓ cups all-purpose flour
½ teaspoon salt
¼ cup plus 3 tablespoons lard or ½ cup
   shortening
3 to 4 tablespoons cold water

Two-Crust Pie; 9-inch

2 cups all-purpose flour
1 teaspoon salt
⅔ cup lard or ⅔ cup plus 2 tablespoons
   shortening
4 to 5 tablespoons cold water

Two-Crust Pie; 10-inch

2⅔ cups all-purpose flour
1 teaspoon salt
¾ cup plus 2 tablespoons lard or 1 cup
   shortening
7 to 8 tablespoons cold water

Mix flour and salt. Cut in lard until particles are size of small peas. Sprinkle with water, 1 tablespoon at a time, tossing with fork until all flour is moistened and pastry almost cleans side of bowl (1 to 2 teaspoons water can be added if necessary).

Gather pastry into ball; shape into flattened round on lightly floured cloth-covered surface. (For Two-Crust Pie, divide pastry in half and shape into 2 rounds.)

Roll pastry 2 inches larger than inverted pie plate with floured cloth-covered rolling pin. Fold pastry into fourths; unfold and ease into plate, pressing firmly against bottom and side.

8 servings per pie pastry

One-Crust Pie; 9-inch:
PER SERVING: Calories 140; Protein 1 g; Carbohydrate 11 g; Fat 10 g; Cholesterol 0 mg; Sodium 70 mg

One-Crust Pie; 10-inch:
PER SERVING: Calories 180; Protein 2 g; Carbohydrate 15 g; Fat 13 g; Cholesterol 0 mg; Sodium 135 mg

Two-Crust Pie; 9-inch:
PER SERVING: Calories 225; Protein 3 g; Carbohydrate 22 g; Fat 14 g; Cholesterol 0 mg; Sodium 275 mg

Two-Crust Pie; 10-inch:
PER SERVING: Calories 360; Protein 4 g; Carbohydrate 29 g; Fat 25 g; Cholesterol 0 mg; Sodium 275 mg

FOR ONE-CRUST PIE: Trim overhanging edge of pastry 1 inch from rim of plate. Fold and roll pastry under, even with plate. Flatten pastry evenly on rim of pie plate. Press firmly around edge with tines of fork, dipping fork into flour occasionally to prevent sticking. Or build up edge of pastry. Place index finger on inside of pastry edge and knuckles (or thumb and index finger) on outside. Pinch pastry into V shape; pinch again to sharpen. Fill and bake as directed in recipe.

FOR BAKED PIE SHELL: Heat oven to 475°. Prick bottom and side thoroughly with fork. Bake 8 to 10 minutes or until light brown; cool.

FOR TWO-CRUST PIE: Turn desired filling into pastry-lined pie plate. Trim overhanging edge of pastry ½ inch from rim of plate. Roll other round of pastry. Fold into fourths; cut slits so steam can escape.

Place over filling and unfold. Trim overhanging edge of pastry 1 inch from rim of plate. Fold and roll top edge under lower edge, pressing on rim to seal. Flatten pastry evenly on rim of pie plate. Press firmly around edge with tines of fork, dipping fork into flour occasionally to prevent sticking. Or build up edge of pastry. Place index finger on inside of pastry edge and knuckles (or thumb and index finger) on outside. Pinch pastry into V shape; pinch again to sharpen.

Country Apple Pie

Apple pie is particularly nice when served with ice cream or a slice of Cheddar cheese.

Pastry for 10-inch Two-Crust Pie (page 47)
1 cup sugar
¼ cup all-purpose flour
¾ teaspoon ground cinnamon
½ teaspoon ground nutmeg
Dash of salt
8 cups thinly sliced pared tart cooking apples (about 8 medium)
4 tablespoons whipping (heavy) cream

Heat oven to 425°. Prepare pastry. Mix sugar, flour, cinnamon, nutmeg and salt. Stir in apples. Turn into pastry-lined deep-dish pie plate, 9 × 1½ inches, or pie plate, 10 × 1½ inches. Drizzle with 3 tablespoons of the whipping cream.

Cover with top crust that has slits cut in it; seal and flute. Brush with remaining whipping cream. Top with leaf or other shapes cut from pastry scraps if desired. Bake 40 to 45 minutes or until crust is brown and juice begins to bubble through slits in crust. **8 servings**

PER SERVING: Calories 570; Protein 5 g; Carbohydrate 79 g; Fat 26 g; Cholesterol 30 mg; Sodium 300 mg

Partridge in a Pear Tree Pie

You can fashion other pastry cutouts for your Christmas pies: Use a cookie cutter (bell, star, tree) or cut around your own patterns.

3 cups (12 ounces) cranberries
1½ cups sugar
1 can (8¾ ounces) crushed pineapple, drained (reserve syrup)
Pastry for 9-inch Two-Crust Pie (page 47)
3 tablespoons flour
¼ teaspoon salt
¼ teaspoon ground cinnamon
1 can (8 ounces) pear halves, drained and cut into halves
Sugar

Cook cranberries, 1½ cups sugar, the pineapple and ¼ cup of the reserved syrup, stirring constantly, until cranberries are tender, about 5 minutes. Cool. Prepare pastry as directed—except flute bottom crust. Mix flour, salt and cinnamon; stir into cranberry mixture. Pour into pastry-lined pie plate. Gently press pear slices spoke-fashion onto cranberry mixture.

Heat oven to 400°. After rolling pastry for top crust, cut partridge, leaf and pear shapes (see photograph). Sprinkle with sugar if desired; place on ungreased cookie sheet. Bake pastry cutouts and pie until cutouts and pie crust are golden brown, 7 to 10 minutes for cutouts and about 40 minutes for pie. Arrange cutouts on pie. **8 servings**

PER SERVING: Calories 465; Protein 4 g; Carbohydrate 74 g; Fat 17 g; Cholesterol 15 mg; Sodium 33 mg

Partridge in a Pear Tree Pie

Pumpkin Pie

9-Inch

Pastry for 9-inch One-Crust Pie (page 47)
2 eggs
½ cup sugar
1 can (16 ounces) pumpkin
1 can (12 ounces) evaporated milk
1 teaspoon ground cinnamon
½ teaspoon salt
½ teaspoon ground ginger
⅛ teaspoon ground cloves

10-Inch

Pastry for 10-inch One-Crust Pie (page 47)
3 eggs
1 cup sugar
2¾ cups canned pumpkin
2¼ cups evaporated milk
1½ teaspoons ground cinnamon
¾ teaspoon salt
¾ teaspoon ground ginger
½ teaspoon ground cloves

Heat oven to 425°. Prepare pastry. Beat eggs slightly with hand beater or wire whisk in medium bowl. Beat in remaining ingredients. To prevent spilling, place pastry-lined pie plate on oven rack. Pour filling into pie plate. Bake 15 minutes.

Reduce oven temperature to 350°. Bake 9-inch pie about 45 minutes longer, 10-inch pie about 55 minutes longer or until knife inserted in center comes out clean. Refrigerate about 4 hours or until chilled. Serve with Sweetened Whipped Cream (page 62) if desired. Immediately refrigerate any remaining pie. **8 servings**

9-Inch
PER SERVING: Calories 285; Protein 6 g; Carbohydrate 32 g; Fat 15 g; Cholesterol 80 mg; Sodium 270 mg

10-Inch
PER SERVING: Calories 430; Protein 10 g; Carbohydrate 53 g; Fat 20 g; Cholesterol 125 mg; Sodium 450 mg

Pumpkin-Honey Pie

Pastry for 9-inch One-Crust Pie (page 47)
3 eggs
2 cups mashed cooked pumpkin*
¾ cup honey
½ cup milk
¼ cup whipping (heavy) cream
1½ teaspoons ground cinnamon
½ teaspoon salt
¼ teaspoon ground ginger
¼ teaspoon ground nutmeg

Heat oven to 400°. Prepare pastry. Beat eggs slightly in large bowl, using hand beater. Beat in remaining ingredients. Pour into pastry-lined pie plate. Cover edge with 2- to 3-inch strip of aluminum foil to prevent excessive browning; remove foil during last 15 minutes of baking.

Bake 50 to 55 minutes or until knife inserted 1 inch from edge comes out clean. Cool 15 minutes; refrigerate until chilled. Serve with sweetened whipped cream sprinkled with nutmeg if desired. Refrigerate any remaining pie.

8 servings

PER SERVING: Calories 315; Protein 5 g; Carbohydrate 45 g; Fat 13 g; Cholesterol 95 mg; Sodium 310 mg

*1 can (16 ounces) pumpkin can be substituted for the mashed cooked pumpkin.

Pumpkin-Honey Pie, Sweet Potato–Pecan Pie (page 52)

Pecan Pie

Pastry for 9-inch One-Crust Pie (page 47)
⅔ cup sugar
⅓ cup margarine or butter, melted
1 cup corn syrup
½ teaspoon salt
3 eggs
1 cup pecan halves or broken pieces

Heat oven to 375°. Prepare pastry. Beat sugar, margarine, corn syrup, salt and eggs with hand beater in medium bowl. Stir in pecans. Pour into pastry-lined pie plate.

Bake 40 to 50 minutes or until set.

8 servings

PER SERVING: Calories 515; Protein 5 g; Carbohydrate 60 g; Fat 30 g; Cholesterol 105 mg; Sodium 350 mg

Sweet Potato-Pecan Pie

A pie for when you can't decide between sweet potato or pecan—here's the best of both worlds!

Pecan Pastry (right)
3 eggs
1¾ cups mashed cooked sweet potatoes*
1 cup sugar
1 cup milk
2 tablespoons butter or margarine, melted
½ teaspoon salt
½ teaspoon ground cinnamon
¼ teaspoon ground nutmeg
⅛ teaspoon ground cloves
½ cup chopped pecans

Heat oven to 425°. Prepare Pecan Pastry. Beat eggs slightly in large bowl, using hand beater. Beat in remaining ingredients except pecans. Pour into pastry-lined pie plate; sprinkle with pecans. Bake 15 minutes.

Reduce oven temperature to 350°. Bake about 45 minutes longer or until knife inserted in center comes out clean. Cool 15 minutes; refrigerate until chilled. Serve with sweetened whipped cream and additional pecans if desired. Refrigerate any remaining pie.　**8 servings**

Pecan Pastry

1 cup all-purpose flour
½ teaspoon salt
⅓ cup lard or ⅓ cup plus 1 tablespoon shortening
2 tablespoons finely chopped pecans
2 to 3 tablespoons cold water

Mix flour and salt. Cut in lard until particles are size of small peas; stir in pecans. Sprinkle with water, 1 tablespoon at a time, tossing with fork until all flour is moistened and pastry almost cleans side of bowl (1 to 2 teaspoons water can be added if necessary).

Gather pastry into a ball; shape into flattened round on lightly floured cloth-covered surface. Roll pastry 2 inches larger than inverted pie plate with floured cloth-covered rolling pin.

Fold pastry into fourths; unfold and ease into plate, pressing firmly against bottom and side. Trim overhanging edge of pastry 1 inch from rim of plate. Fold and roll pastry under, even with plate; build up a high edge and flute.

PER SERVING: Calories 420; Protein 6 g; Carbohydrate 54 g; Fat 20 g; Cholesterol 100 mg; Sodium 330 mg

*1¾ cups mashed canned sweet potatoes can be substituted for the mashed cooked sweet potatoes.

Peppermint Stick Pie

Chocolate Cookie Crust (below)
24 large marshmallows
½ cup milk
1 teaspoon vanilla
⅛ teaspoon salt
6 drops peppermint extract
6 drops red food color
1 cup whipping (heavy) cream
2 tablespoons crushed peppermint candy

Bake Chocolate Cookie Crust. Heat marshmallows and milk over low heat, stirring constantly, just until marshmallows are melted. Remove from heat; stir in vanilla, salt, peppermint extract and food color. Refrigerate, stirring occasionally, until mixture mounds slightly when dropped from a spoon.

Beat whipping cream in chilled bowl until stiff. Stir marshmallow mixture until blended; fold into whipped cream. Pour into crust. Refrigerate at least 12 hours. Just before serving, sprinkle with crushed candy. **8 servings**

Chocolate Cookie Crust

Heat oven to 350°. Mix 1½ cups chocolate wafer crumbs and ¼ cup margarine or butter, melted. Press firmly against bottom and side of ungreased 9-inch pie plate. Bake 10 minutes. Cool.

PER SERVING: Calories 385; Protein 4 g; Carbohydrate 45 g; Fat 21 g; Cholesterol 37 mg; Sodium 350 mg

Chocolate Angel Pie

Meringue makes a light, crisp and slightly chewy shell for angel pies.

4 egg whites
¼ teaspoon cream of tartar
⅛ teaspoon salt
¾ cup sugar
1 teaspoon vanilla
½ cup chopped pecans
1 package (6 ounces) semisweet chocolate chips (1 cup)
¼ cup whipping (heavy) cream
1½ teaspoons vanilla
1½ cups whipping (heavy) cream

Heat oven to 275°. Generously grease pie plate, 9 × 1¼ inches; grease top edge of pie plate. Beat egg whites, cream of tartar and salt in small bowl until foamy. Beat in sugar, 1 tablespoon at a time; continue beating until stiff and glossy. Do not underbeat. Beat in vanilla; fold in pecans. Spread on bottom and up side of pie plate, using back of spoon and building up 1-inch edge to form shell. Bake 1½ hours. Turn oven off. Leave shell in oven with door closed 1 hour. Remove from oven and cool completely.

Heat chocolate chips and ¼ cup whipping cream in saucepan over low heat, stirring frequently, until chocolate is melted. Cool 30 minutes.

Stir in vanilla. Beat 1½ cups whipping cream in chilled medium bowl until stiff. Fold chocolate mixture into whipped cream. Spoon into meringue shell. Cover and refrigerate at least 12 hours but no longer than 24 hours. Garnish with whipped cream, chopped nuts or grated chocolate if desired. Refrigerate any remaining pie. **12 servings**

PER SERVING: Calories 270; Protein 3 g; Carbohydrate 24 g; Fat 18 g; Cholesterol 40 mg; Sodium 60 mg

Classic French Silk Pie

Classic French Silk Pie

We have a new method for making this classic pie—cooking the eggs—which gives the filling a soft texture. Freezing the pie makes it easier to cut, yet it still retains its rich, smooth texture and great chocolate flavor.

Pastry for 9-inch One-Crust Pie Shell (page 47)
¼ cup (½ stick) margarine or butter, softened
3 ounces unsweetened chocolate
1 cup sugar
2 tablespoons cornstarch
3 eggs
1 teaspoon vanilla
1 cup chilled whipping (heavy) cream
Whipped cream, if desired

Prepare and bake Pie Shell; cool. Heat margarine and chocolate in 2-quart saucepan over low heat until melted. Remove from heat. Mix sugar and cornstarch; stir into chocolate mixture. Meanwhile, beat eggs in small bowl on medium speed until thick and lemon colored; stir into chocolate mixture. Cook mixture over medium heat 5 minutes, stirring constantly, until thick and glossy; stir in vanilla. Cool 10 minutes, stirring occasionally.

Beat whipping cream in chilled medium bowl until stiff. Fold chocolate mixture into whipped cream; pour into Pie Shell. Cover and freeze about 4 hours or until firm. Garnish with whipped cream. Freeze any remaining pie.

10 servings

PER SERVING; Calories 375; Protein 4 g; Carbohydrate 34 g; Fat 25 g; Cholesterol 95 mg; Sodium 190 mg

Crunchy Nut Ice Cream Pie

Have fun choosing the ice cream flavor for this pie and, if you like, use a different sauce, such as caramel, to complement the ice cream.

1½ cups ground pecans, walnuts or almonds
3 tablespoons sugar
2 tablespoons margarine or butter, softened
1 quart coffee, chocolate or vanilla ice cream
Rich Chocolate Sauce (below)

Heat oven to 400°. Mix pecans, sugar and margarine. Press firmly and evenly against bottom and side of ungreased pie plate, 9 × 1¼ inches. Bake 6 to 8 minutes; cool.

Spoon or scoop ice cream into pie shell. Freeze until firm, about 4 hours. Remove from freezer 10 to 15 minutes before serving. Cut into wedges; spoon Rich Chocolate Sauce over each serving. **8 servings**

Rich Chocolate Sauce

8 ounces sweet cooking chocolate or 1 package (6 ounces) semisweet chocolate chips (1 cup)
¼ cup sugar
¼ cup water
¼ cup half-and-half

Heat chocolate, sugar and water in saucepan over low heat, stirring constantly, until chocolate and sugar are melted. Remove from heat; blend in half-and-half. Serve warm or cool.

PER SERVING: Calories 505; Protein 5 g; Carbohydrate 51 g; Fat 31 g; Cholesterol 25 mg; Sodium 90 mg

Hazelnut Chocolate Torte

4

Tortes, Tarts and Other Treats

Hazelnut Chocolate Torte

6 eggs, separated
1 tablespoon finely shredded orange peel
¾ teaspoon ground cinnamon
½ cup granulated sugar
1 teaspoon cream of tartar
½ cup granulated sugar
3 cups very finely ground hazelnuts
½ cup all-purpose flour
Chocolate Butter Frosting (right)
1 cup chilled whipping (heavy) cream
½ cup powdered sugar
¼ cup cocoa
2 teaspoons finely shredded orange peel
½ cup chopped hazelnuts

Heat oven to 325°. Grease bottom only of springform pan, 9 × 3 inches. Line bottom with waxed paper; grease generously. Beat egg yolks, 1 tablespoon orange peel and the cinnamon in 1½-quart bowl on high speed until very thick and light colored, about 6 minutes. Gradually beat in ½ cup granulated sugar, 1 tablespoon at a time; reserve. Wash beaters.

Beat egg whites and cream of tartar in 2½-quart bowl on high speed until soft peaks form. Gradually beat in ½ cup granulated sugar, 1 tablespoon at a time. Continue beating until stiff peaks form. Fold egg yolk mixture into meringue. Mix 3 cups ground hazelnuts and the flour. Sprinkle about ⅓ of the hazelnut mixture over meringue; fold in. Repeat with remaining hazelnut mixture. Spread in pan.

Bake until wooden pick inserted in center comes out clean, 55 to 60 minutes; cool on wire rack 15 minutes. Loosen side of cake from pan.

Carefully remove side of pan. Invert cake on wire rack; remove bottom of pan. Turn cake right side up. Cool cake completely. Wrap tightly; refrigerate at least 4 hours for easier slicing.

Prepare Chocolate Butter Frosting. Reserve 1 cup for decorating. Beat whipping cream, powdered sugar and cocoa in chilled 1½-quart bowl until stiff. Fold in 2 teaspoons orange peel. Carefully split cake horizontally to make 3 layers. Spread 1 layer with half of the whipped cream mixture; repeat. Top with remaining layer. Frost side and top of torte with Chocolate Butter Frosting. Press ½ cup hazelnuts around side.

Place reserved 1 cup Chocolate Butter Frosting in decorating bag with large open star tip #4B. Pipe large rosettes on top of cake. Garnish with whole hazelnuts if desired. Refrigerate at least 8 hours. Refrigerate any remaining torte.

16 servings

Chocolate Butter Frosting

½ cup margarine or butter, softened
3 squares (1 ounce each) unsweetened chocolate, melted and cooled, or ½ cup cocoa
3 cups powdered sugar
1 tablespoon brandy, if desired
2 teaspoons vanilla
About 3 tablespoons milk

Beat margarine and chocolate. Beat in remaining ingredients until of spreading consistency.

PER SERVING: Calories 435; Protein 6 g; Carbohydrate 47 g; Fat 25 g; Cholesterol 95 mg; Sodium 110 mg

Nut Cracker Sweet Torte

6 eggs, separated
½ cup sugar
2 tablespoons vegetable oil
1 tablespoon rum flavoring
½ cup sugar
¼ cup all-purpose flour
1¼ teaspoons baking powder
1 teaspoon ground cinnamon
½ teaspoon ground cloves
1 cup fine graham cracker crumbs (about 12 squares)
1 cup finely chopped nuts
1 square (1 ounce) unsweetened chocolate, grated
Rum-flavored Whipped Cream (right)

Heat oven to 350°. Line bottoms of 2 round pans, 8 × 1½ or 9 × 1½ inches, with aluminum foil. Beat egg whites in 2½-quart bowl until frothy. Beat in ½ cup sugar, 1 tablespoon at a time; continue beating until stiff. Beat egg yolks, oil and rum flavoring in 1½-quart bowl on low speed until blended. Add ½ cup sugar, the flour, baking powder, cinnamon and cloves; beat on medium speed 1 minute. Fold in crumbs, nuts and chocolate. Pour into pans.

Bake until top springs back when touched lightly, 30 to 35 minutes. Cool 10 minutes. Loosen edges of layers with knife; invert pan and hit sharply on table. (Cake will drop out.) Remove foil; cool completely.

Split cake to make 4 layers. Fill layers and frost top of torte with Rum-flavored Whipped Cream. Garnish with grated chocolate or chocolate curls if desired. Refrigerate torte at least 8 hours but no longer than 24 hours. (Torte mellows and becomes moist with refrigeration.)

12 servings

Rum-flavored Whipped Cream

Beat 2 cups chilled whipping (heavy) cream, ½ cup powdered sugar and 2 teaspoons rum flavoring in chilled 1½-quart bowl until stiff.

PER SERVING: Calories 390; Protein 6 g; Carbohydrate 34 g; Fat 25 g; Cholesterol 150 mg; Sodium 130 mg

Easy Walnut Torte

1½ cups chopped walnuts
1½ cups vanilla wafer crumbs
1 cup packed brown sugar
1 cup margarine or butter, melted
1 package (18.25 ounces) devil's food cake mix with pudding
1½ cups chilled whipping (heavy) cream
3 tablespoons granulated sugar
1 teaspoon vanilla

Heat oven to 350°. Mix walnuts, wafer crumbs, brown sugar and margarine. Spread about ¾ cup in each of 2 ungreased round pans, 9 × 1½ inches. Prepare cake mix as directed on package. Pour about 1¼ cups batter over walnut mixture in each pan; refrigerate remaining batter.

Bake until top springs back when touched lightly, about 20 minutes. Immediately remove from pans; invert. Repeat with remaining batter and walnut mixture. Cool layers completely.

Beat whipping cream, granulated sugar and vanilla in chilled 1½-quart bowl until stiff. Place 1 layer, walnut side up, on serving plate; spread with whipped cream. Repeat with remaining layers and whipped cream. Frost top of torte with whipped cream. Refrigerate. **16 servings**

PER SERVING: Calories 585; Protein 5 g; Carbohydrate 62 g; Fat 35 g; Cholesterol 35 mg; Sodium 560 mg

Angel Meringue Torte

A pretty red-and-white torte for Christmas.

6 egg whites
½ teaspoon cream of tartar
¼ teaspoon salt
1½ cups sugar
½ teaspoon vanilla
½ teaspoon almond extract
1 cup whipping (heavy) cream
Cranberries Jubilee (right) or sweetened
sliced strawberries

Heat oven to 450°. Butter bottom only of 9-inch springform pan or tube pan, 10 × 4 inches. Beat egg whites, cream of tartar and salt in large mixer bowl on medium speed until foamy. On high speed beat in sugar, 2 tablespoons at a time; beat until stiff and glossy. Beat in vanilla and almond extract. Do not underbeat. Spread evenly in pan. Place in oven; immediately turn off oven. Leave pan in oven at least 8 hours.

Run knife around torte to loosen; invert on serving plate. Beat whipping cream in chilled bowl until stiff. Frost torte with whipped cream. Refrigerate at least 4 hours. Cut into wedges and serve with Cranberries Jubilee. Refrigerate any remaining torte.   **12 servings**

Cranberries Jubilee

¾ teaspoon grated orange peel
½ cup orange juice
½ cup water
2 cups sugar
2 cups cranberries
2 tablespoons water
2 teaspoons cornstarch
¼ cup brandy

Mix orange peel, orange juice, ½ cup water and the sugar in 2-quart saucepan. Heat to boiling; boil 5 minutes. Stir in cranberries. Heat to boiling; boil rapidly 5 minutes. Mix 2 tablespoons water and the cornstarch; stir into cranberry mixture. Cook, stirring constantly, until mixture thickens and boils. Boil and stir 1 minute.

Pour cranberry mixture into chafing dish to keep warm. Heat brandy in saucepan until warm; ignite and pour over cranberry mixture.

PER SERVING: Calories 370; Protein 2 g; Carbohydrate 78 g; Fat 6 g; Cholesterol 20 mg; Sodium 100 mg

Frozen Torte

Frozen Torte

4 egg whites
½ teaspoon cream of tartar
1 cup sugar
Mocha Filling (below)

Heat oven to 275°. Cover 2 cookie sheets with heavy brown paper. Beat egg whites and cream of tartar in large bowl on high speed until foamy. Beat in sugar, 1 tablespoon at a time; continue beating until stiff and glossy. Do not underbeat.

Divide meringue into 3 parts. Place 1 part on 1 cookie sheet; shape into 6-inch circle. Place remaining 2 parts on second cookie sheet; shape each part into 6-inch circle. Bake 45 minutes. Turn off oven; leave meringues in oven with door closed 1 hour. Remove from oven; finish cooling meringues away from draft.

Stack meringues, spreading Mocha Filling between layers; frost top of torte with filling. Decorate with shaved chocolate if desired. Freeze uncovered at least 3 hours or until filling on top is firm. (For ease in cutting, dip knife into hot water and wipe after cutting each slice.) Freeze any remaining torte. **6 servings**

Mocha Filling

¼ cup sugar
3 tablespoons cocoa
2 tablespoons powdered instant coffee
2 cups whipping (heavy) cream

Beat all ingredients in chilled medium bowl until stiff.

PER SERVING: Calories 470; Protein 4 g; Carbohydrate 46 g; Fat 30 g; Cholesterol 110 mg; Sodium 85 mg

Brown Sugar Pear Tart

A quick and satisfying tart, perfect to bake during the busy holiday season.

Pecan Crust (below)
3 or 4 medium pears (about 2 pounds), pared
½ cup packed brown sugar
1 tablespoon all-purpose flour
½ teaspoon ground cinnamon
1 tablespoon margarine or butter

Bake Pecan Crust. Cut each pear lengthwise into halves; remove core. Place each pear half, cut side down, on cutting surface. Cut crosswise into thin slices. With spatula, lift each pear half and arrange on crust, separating and overlapping slices (retain pear shape) to cover surface of crust.

Mix brown sugar, flour, cinnamon and margarine; sprinkle over pears. Bake in 375° oven until crust is golden brown and pears are tender, 15 to 20 minutes. **6 servings**

Pecan Crust

1⅓ cups all-purpose flour
⅓ cup packed brown sugar
⅓ cup finely chopped pecans
½ teaspoon ground nutmeg
½ teaspoon grated lemon peel
⅔ cup margarine or butter, softened

Heat oven to 375°. Mix all ingredients except margarine; cut in margarine until crumbly. Press firmly and evenly against bottom and side of ungreased 12-inch pizza pan. Bake 8 minutes.

PER SERVING: Calories 520; Protein 4 g; Carbohydrate 66 g; Fat 27 g; Cholesterol 0 mg; Sodium 270 mg

Red Currant–glazed Grape Tart

1½ cups all-purpose flour
⅔ cup butter or margarine, softened
⅓ cup sugar
3 cups seedless red grape halves
1 envelope unflavored gelatin
¼ cup orange juice
1 jar (10 ounces) red currant jelly

Heat oven to 400°. Mix flour, butter and sugar until crumbly. Press firmly and evenly in bottom of 12-inch pizza pan. Bake 10 to 15 minutes or until light brown; cool.

Place grapes evenly over crust. Sprinkle gelatin on orange juice in 1-quart saucepan to soften. Stir in jelly. Heat over medium heat, stirring constantly, until gelatin is dissolved and jelly is melted. Spoon over grapes. Refrigerate about 1½ hours or until set. Serve with sweetened whipped cream if desired. **10 servings**

PER SERVING: Calories 256; Protein 3 g; Carbohydrate 44 g; Fat 12 g; Cholesterol 0 mg; Sodium 155 mg

Cream Puffs

Cream puffs are always a treat, and the array of whipped cream fillings below makes them even more tempting.

1 cup water
½ cup butter or margarine
1 cup all-purpose flour
4 eggs
Whipped Cream Fillings (right)
Powdered sugar

Heat oven to 400°. Heat water and butter to rolling boil in 2½-quart saucepan. Stir in flour. Stir vigorously over low heat about 1 minute or until mixture forms a ball; remove from heat. Beat in eggs, all at once; continue beating until smooth. Drop dough by scant ¼ cupfuls about 3 inches apart onto ungreased cookie sheet.

Bake 35 to 40 minutes or until puffed and golden. Cool on wire rack away from draft. Cut off tops; pull out any filaments of soft dough. Fill puffs with one of the Whipped Cream Fillings. Replace tops; dust with powdered sugar. Serve immediately or refrigerate up to 4 hours.
10 cream puffs

Whipped Cream Fillings

Sweetened Whipped Cream. Beat 1 cup whipping (heavy) cream, ¼ cup powdered sugar and ½ teaspoon vanilla in chilled bowl until stiff.
enough filling for 6 puffs

Tropical Whipped Cream. Beat 1 cup whipping (heavy) cream, ¼ cup powdered sugar and ½ teaspoon vanilla in chilled bowl until stiff. Fold in ⅓ cup crushed pineapple, well drained, ⅓ cup chopped toasted almonds and ⅓ cup flaked coconut. **enough filling for 10 puffs**

Spiced Whipped Cream. Beat 1 cup whipping (heavy) cream, ¼ cup powdered sugar, ½ teaspoon ground cinnamon or ground nutmeg or ¼ teaspoon ground ginger and ½ teaspoon vanilla in chilled bowl until stiff.
enough filling for 10 puffs

PER SERVING: Calories 240; Protein 4 g; Carbohydrate 14 g; Fat 19 g; Cholesterol 110 mg; Sodium 140 mg

Chocolate Cheese Eclairs

¾ cup plus 2 tablespoons all-purpose
   flour
2 tablespoons cocoa
1 tablespoon sugar
1 cup water
½ cup margarine or butter
4 eggs
Chocolate Cheese Filling (right)
Cocoa Glaze (right)

Heat oven to 400°. Mix flour, cocoa and sugar. Heat water and margarine in 3-quart saucepan to a rolling boil. Stir in flour mixture. Stir vigorously over low heat until mixture forms a ball, about 1 minute. Remove from heat. Beat in eggs; continue beating until smooth. Drop dough by about ¼ cupfuls 3 inches apart onto ungreased cookie sheet. With spatula, shape each into finger 4½ inches long and 1½ inches wide. Bake until puffed and darker brown on top, 35 to 40 minutes; cool.

Cut off tops; pull out any filaments of soft dough. Fill éclairs with Chocolate Cheese Filling; replace tops. Spread with Cocoa Glaze just before serving. Refrigerate any remaining éclairs.

8 éclairs

Chocolate Cheese Filling

¼ cup semisweet chocolate chips
1 package (3 ounces) cream cheese,
   softened
⅓ cup packed brown sugar
¼ cup milk
½ teaspoon vanilla
1 cup chilled whipping (heavy) cream

Heat chocolate chips in small heavy saucepan over low heat, stirring occasionally, until melted; cool. Beat cream cheese, brown sugar, milk and vanilla until smooth and creamy. Stir in chocolate. Beat whipping cream in chilled bowl until soft peaks form. Fold in chocolate mixture.

Cocoa Glaze

Mix 1 cup powdered sugar and 2 tablespoons cocoa. Stir in 2 tablespoons milk until smooth. If necessary, stir in additional milk, ½ teaspoon at a time, until of desired consistency.

PER SERVING: Calories 460; Protein 7 g; Carbohydrate 43 g; Fat 29 g; Cholesterol 150 mg; Sodium 220 mg

Lindy's Cheesecake

1 cup all-purpose flour
½ cup margarine or butter, softened
¼ cup sugar
1 tablespoon grated lemon peel
1 egg yolk
5 packages (8 ounces each) cream cheese, softened
1¾ cups sugar
3 tablespoons all-purpose flour
1 tablespoon grated orange peel
1 tablespoon grated lemon peel
¼ teaspoon salt
5 eggs
2 egg yolks
¼ cup whipping (heavy) cream
¾ cup whipping (heavy) cream
⅓ cup toasted slivered almonds, if desired

Move oven rack to lowest position. Heat oven to 400°. Lightly grease springform pan, 9 × 3 inches; remove bottom. Mix 1 cup flour, the margarine, ¼ cup sugar, 1 tablespoon lemon peel and 1 egg yolk with hands. Press one-third of the mixture evenly on bottom of pan. Place on cookie sheet. Bake 8 to 10 minutes or until golden brown; cool. Assemble bottom and side of pan; secure side. Press remaining mixture all the way up side of pan.

Heat oven to 475°. Beat cream cheese, 1¾ cups sugar, 3 tablespoons flour, the orange peel, 1 tablespoon lemon peel, the salt and 2 eggs in large bowl until smooth. Continue beating, adding remaining eggs and 2 egg yolks, one at a time, until blended. Beat in ¼ cup whipping cream on low speed. Pour into pan. Bake 15 minutes. Reduce oven temperature to 200°. Bake 1 hour. Turn off oven and leave cheesecake in oven 15 minutes. Run metal spatula along side of cheesecake to loosen before and after refrigerating. Cover and refrigerate at least 12 hours.

Remove cheesecake from side of pan. Beat ¾ cup whipping cream in chilled bowl until stiff. Spread whipped cream over top of cheesecake. Decorate with almonds. Refrigerate any remaining cheesecake. **20 servings**

Lindy's Cheesecake Squares

Heat oven to 400°. Lightly grease rectangular pan, 13 × 9 × 2 inches. Press crust mixture on bottom of pan. Do not place pan on cookie sheet. Bake 15 minutes; cool. Heat oven to 475°. Pour cream cheese mixture into pan. Bake 15 minutes. Reduce oven temperature to 200°. Bake about 45 minutes or until center is set. Turn off oven and leave cheesecake in oven 15 minutes; cool 15 minutes. Cover and refrigerate at least 12 hours.

Continue as directed—except increase almonds to ½ cup.

PER SERVING: Calories 410; Protein 7 g; Carbohydrate 26 g; Fat 31 g; Cholesterol 165 mg; Sodium 300 mg

Signature Holiday Cheesecake

It's easy to make your own personal, holiday cheesecake.

Melt one ounce of unsweetened or semisweet chocolate. Pour into a small plastic bag. Snip off just the tip of one corner of the bag, and write a holiday message on top of the cheesecake

Flatten large green gumdrops by rolling them in sugar. Cut to resemble holly leaves; arrange on cheesecake. Add red cinnamon candies for holly berries. Serve cheesecake on a holiday plate for extra cheer, if you wish.

Pumpkin Cheesecake

A wonderful variation on cheesecake, which could easily become a favorite Thanksgiving dessert.

1½ cups graham cracker crumbs
½ cup finely chopped pecans
⅓ cup packed brown sugar
½ cup margarine or butter, melted
3 packages (8 ounces each) cream cheese, softened
½ cup sour cream
1 cup packed brown sugar
2 teaspoons ground cinnamon
½ teaspoon ground nutmeg
½ teaspoon ground ginger
¼ teaspoon ground allspice
1 can (16 ounces) pumpkin
3 eggs
Caramelized Sugar (right)

Mix graham cracker crumbs, pecans, ⅓ cup brown sugar and the margarine. Press evenly on bottom and sides of ungreased springform pan, 9 × 3 inches. Refrigerate 20 minutes.

Heat oven to 300°. Beat cream cheese, sour cream, 1 cup brown sugar and the spices in large bowl on medium speed until smooth. Add pumpkin. Beat in eggs on low speed. Pour over crumb mixture. Bake about 1 hour 15 minutes or until center is firm. Cover and refrigerate at least 3 hours but no longer than 48 hours.

Prepare Caramelized Sugar; drizzle with fork over top of chilled cheesecake. Loosen cheesecake from side of pan; remove side of pan. Place cheesecake on plate. Refrigerate any remaining cheesecake immediately.

20 servings

Caramelized Sugar

1 cup sugar
3 tablespoons water

Combine sugar and water in small saucepan. Boil mixture over medium heat, stirring until sugar is dissolved. Boil syrup, without stirring, until golden brown. Remove from heat and gently swirl until syrup stops cooking. Let caramel cool about 1 minute or until thick enough to drizzle from fork.

PER SERVING: Calories 340; Protein 4 g; Carbohydrate 33 g; Fat 21 g; Cholesterol 75 mg; Sodium 220 mg

Bittersweet Chocolate Cheesecake with White Truffle Sauce

2 packages (8 ounces each) cream cheese, softened
1 teaspoon vanilla
⅔ cup sugar
1 tablespoon all-purpose flour
3 eggs
8 ounces bittersweet chocolate, melted and cooled
White Truffle Sauce (below)

Heat oven to 275°. Lightly grease springform pan, 9 × 3 inches. Beat cream cheese and vanilla on medium speed in medium bowl until smooth. Gradually add sugar, beating until fluffy. Beat in flour. Beat in eggs, one at a time. Beat in chocolate; pour into pan.

Bake about 1 hour 15 minutes or until center is firm. Cool 15 minutes. Run metal spatula along side of cheesecake to loosen before and after refrigerating. Cover and refrigerate about 3 hours or until chilled. Meanwhile, prepare White Truffle Sauce.

Remove cheesecake from side of pan. Let cheesecake stand at room temperature 15 minutes before cutting. Serve cheesecake with sauce and, if desired, fresh raspberries or strawberries. Refrigerate any remaining cheesecake. **12 servings**

White Truffle Sauce

1 package (6 ounces) white baking bar, chopped
2 tablespoons margarine or butter
½ cup whipping (heavy) cream

Heat baking bar and margarine in heavy 2-quart saucepan over low heat, stirring constantly, until melted (mixture will be thick and grainy); remove from heat. Stir in whipping cream until smooth. Cover and refrigerate about 2 hours or until chilled.

PER SERVING: Calories 415; Protein 7 g; Carbohydrate 27 g; Fat 34 g; Cholesterol 110 mg; Sodium 155 mg

Chocolate Terrine

This luscious dessert takes its name from the pan it was cooked in. We use a loaf pan for this elegant treat with wonderful results.

1 package (3½ ounces) almond paste
1½ cups half-and-half
4 squares (1 ounce each) semisweet chocolate, coarsely chopped
4 ounces white chocolate (vanilla-flavored candy coating), coarsely chopped
4 eggs, slightly beaten
2 tablespoons brandy
Chocolate Glaze (right)

Line loaf pan, 8½ × 4½ × 2½ inches, with aluminum foil, leaving about 2 inches overhanging sides. Roll almond paste between 2 sheets waxed paper into rectangle, 8 × 4 inches; cover with plastic wrap and set aside.

Heat oven to 350°. Heat half-and-half, semisweet chocolate and white chocolate over low heat, stirring constantly, until chocolates are melted and mixture is smooth; cool slightly. Gradually stir eggs and brandy into chocolate mixture. Pour into lined pan.

Place pan in pan of very hot water (1 inch deep) in oven. Bake until knife inserted halfway between edge and center comes out clean, 40 to 50 minutes. Remove from water. Remove waxed paper from almond paste and immediately place on hot terrine; cool 1 hour. Cover and refrigerate at least 6 hours but no longer than 24 hours.

Prepare Chocolate Glaze; reserve ¼ cup. Remove terrine from pan by inverting on serving plate. Carefully remove foil. Spread remaining glaze evenly and smoothly over sides and top of terrine.

Stir 1 to 2 tablespoons powdered sugar into reserved chocolate glaze until smooth and of desired consistency. Place in decorating bag with small writing tip or small sturdy plastic storage bag. (If using plastic bag, cut off very small corner of bag, about ⅛ inch in diameter.) Write *Terrine* on top and decorate around edges of top with remaining chocolate. To serve, cut into 8 slices, about 1 inch each; cut slices into halves. Refrigerate any remaining terrine.

16 servings

Chocolate Glaze

Heat 1 cup semisweet chocolate chips, ¼ cup margarine or butter and 2 tablespoons corn syrup over low heat, stirring constantly, until chocolate is melted; cool.

PER SERVING: Calories 250; Protein 4 g; Carbohydrate 22 g; Fat 16 g; Cholesterol 60 mg; Sodium 70 mg

Chocolate Soufflé

⅓ cup sugar
⅓ cup cocoa
¼ cup all-purpose flour
1 cup milk
3 egg yolks
2 tablespoons margarine or butter, softened
1 teaspoon vanilla
4 egg whites
¼ teaspoon cream of tartar
⅛ teaspoon salt
3 tablespoons sugar
Creamy Sauce (right)

Mix ⅓ cup sugar, the cocoa and flour in 1-quart saucepan. Stir in milk gradually. Heat, stirring constantly, until mixture boils. Remove from heat. Beat yolks in 1½-quart bowl with fork. Beat in about one-third of cocoa mixture. Stir in remaining cocoa mixture gradually. Stir in margarine and vanilla. Cool slightly.

Place oven rack in lowest position. Heat oven to 350°. Butter and sugar 6-cup soufflé dish. Make 4-inch brand of triple thickness aluminum foil 2 inches longer than circumference of dish. Butter and sugar one side of foil band. Extend height of soufflé dish 2 inches by securing foil band buttered side in around outside edge of dish.

Beat egg whites, cream of tartar and salt in 2½-quart bowl until foamy. Beat in 3 tablespoons sugar, 1 tablespoon at a time; continue beating until stiff and glossy. Do not underbeat. Stir about one-fourth of the egg whites into chocolate mixture. Fold in remaining whites. Pour carefully into soufflé dish. Place dish in square pan, 9 × 9 × 2 inches, on oven rack; pour very hot water (1 inch deep) into pan. Bake 1 hour 15 minutes. Serve immediately with Creamy Sauce.

6 servings

Creamy Sauce

Heat ½ cup powdered sugar, ½ cup margarine or butter and ½ cup whipping (heavy) cream to boiling in 1-quart saucepan over medium heat, stirring occasionally.

PER SERVING: Calories 370; Protein 7 g; Carbohydrate 36 g; Fat 22 g; Cholesterol 130 mg; Sodium 260 mg

Tipsy Squire

Known variously as tipsy pudding, tipsy parson and squire cake, Tipsy Squire is a version of its liquor-soaked British antecedent, trifle. This simple cake is cut in wedges, which are then split and reassembled with Sherry Custard Sauce, whipped cream and toasted almonds. Marsala, rum, cognac or whiskey may be substituted for the sherry in the sauce.

1¼ **cups cake flour**
1 **teaspoon baking powder**
3 **eggs**
1 **cup sugar**
½ **cup warm milk**
½ **teaspoon vanilla**
¼ **cup butter or margarine, melted**
Sherry Custard Sauce (right)
½ **cup whipping (heavy) cream**
½ **cup slivered almonds, toasted**

Heat oven to 350°. Line bottom of square pan, 9 × 9 × 2 inches, with waxed paper. Mix flour and baking powder; reserve. Beat eggs and sugar in large bowl on high speed about 3 minutes or until thick and lemon colored. Beat in milk and vanilla on low speed. Beat in flour mixture; stir in butter carefully. Pour into pan.

Bake about 25 minutes or until wooden pick inserted in center comes out clean. Cool 10 minutes; remove from pan and cool completely. Prepare Sherry Custard Sauce. Beat whipping cream in chilled bowl until stiff. Cut cake into serving pieces; split each piece horizontally into halves. Place bottom half on serving plate; top with 3 tablespoons custard sauce. Cover with other half; top with 2 to 3 tablespoons custard sauce. Garnish with whipped cream and almonds. **9 servings**

Sherry Custard Sauce

2 **eggs**
2 **egg yolks**
⅓ **cup sugar**
Dash of salt
2½ **cups milk**
2 **tablespoons sherry**

Mix eggs, egg yolks, sugar and salt in heavy 2-quart saucepan. Stir in milk gradually. Cook over medium-low heat, stirring constantly, just to boiling; remove from heat. Stir in sherry. Pour into glass or plastic bowl. Cover and refrigerate at least 2 hours but no longer than 24 hours.

PER SERVING: Calories 390; Protein 9 g; Carbohydrate 48 g; Fat 18 g; Cholesterol 200 mg; Sodium 190 mg

Peanut Brittle Bread Pudding

4 **cups soft bread cubes (4 to 5 slices bread)**
½ **cup coarsely broken peanut brittle**
½ **cup semisweet chocolate chips**
1 **egg**
½ **cup milk**
½ **cup packed brown sugar**
¼ **cup margarine or butter, melted**
1 **cup chilled whipping (heavy) cream**
¼ **cup chocolate-flavored syrup**

Heat oven to 350°. Place 2 cups of the bread cubes in greased 1-quart casserole. Sprinkle with half of the peanut brittle and half of the chocolate chips; repeat with remaining bread cubes, peanut brittle and chocolate chips. Beat egg; stir in milk, brown sugar and margarine. Pour over bread mixture. Bake 30 minutes.

Beat whipping cream and syrup in 1-quart chilled bowl until soft peaks form. Serve with warm pudding. **6 servings**

PER SERVING: Calories 490; Protein 6 g; Carbohydrate 52 g; Fat 29 g; Cholesterol 80 mg; Sodium 250 mg

Tipsy Squire

Brandy Flans

¾ **cup sugar**
2 **tablespoons water**
½ **cup sugar**
2 **eggs, slightly beaten**
2 **tablespoons brandy or 2 teaspoons**
   brandy flavoring
½ **teaspoon vanilla**
¼ **teaspoon ground nutmeg**
¼ **teaspoon ground cinnamon**
¼ **teaspoon ground allspice**
Dash of salt
2 **cups milk, scalded and cooled**

Heat ¾ cup sugar in heavy 1-quart saucepan over low heat, stirring constantly, until sugar is melted and golden brown. Gradually stir in water. Divide syrup evenly among six 6-ounce custard cups. Allow syrup to harden in cups about 10 minutes.

Heat oven to 350°. Mix ½ cup sugar, the eggs, brandy, vanilla, nutmeg, cinnamon, allspice and salt. Gradually stir in milk. Pour custard mixture over syrup. Place cups in rectangular pan, 13 × 9 × 2 inches, on oven rack. Pour very hot water into pan to within ½ inch of tops of cups.

Bake about 45 minutes or until knife inserted halfway between center and edge comes out clean. Remove cups from water. Refrigerate until chilled; unmold at serving time.

6 servings

PER SERVING: Calories 225; Protein 4 g; Carbohydrate 46 g; Fat 3 g; Cholesterol 80 mg; Sodium 60 mg

Chocolate Pots de Crème

⅔ **cup semisweet chocolate chips**
1 **cup half-and-half**
3 **tablespoons sugar**
2 **tablespoons rum, if desired**
Dash of salt
2 **eggs**

Heat oven to 350°. Heat chocolate chips and half-and-half in 1½-quart saucepan over medium heat, stirring constantly, until chocolate is melted and mixture is smooth; cool slightly. Beat remaining ingredients. Gradually stir into chocolate mixture. Pour into four 6-ounce custard cups or 4 or 5 ovenproof pot de crème cups.

Place cups in baking pan on oven rack. Pour boiling water into pan to within ½ inch of tops of cups. Bake 20 minutes; cool slightly. Cover and refrigerate at least 4 hours. Refrigerate any remaining pudding. **4 or 5 servings**

PER SERVING: Calories 315; Protein 6 g; Carbohydrate 29 g; Fat 18 g; Cholesterol 130 mg; Sodium 60 mg

Plum Pudding

1 cup milk
3 cups soft bread crumbs
½ cup shortening, melted
½ cup molasses
1 cup all-purpose flour
½ cup chopped raisins
½ cup finely chopped citron
2 teaspoons ground cinnamon
1 teaspoon baking soda
½ teaspoon salt
¼ teaspoon ground allspice
¼ teaspoon ground cloves
Amber Sauce (below) or Sherried Hard
    Sauce (right)

Generously grease 4-cup mold. Pour milk over bread crumbs in large bowl. Mix in shortening and molasses. Stir in remaining ingredients except Amber Sauce. Pour into mold. Cover with aluminum foil.

Place mold on rack in Dutch oven. Pour in boiling water up to level of rack. Cover and heat to boiling. Keep water boiling over low heat 3 hours or until wooden pick inserted in center comes out clean. (If it is necessary to add water during steaming, lift cover and quickly add boiling water.) Unmold pudding; cut into slices. Serve warm with Amber Sauce.   **8 servings**

Amber Sauce

1 cup packed brown sugar
½ cup light corn syrup
½ cup half-and-half
¼ cup butter or margarine

Mix all ingredients in 1-quart saucepan. Cook over low heat 5 minutes, stirring occasionally. Serve warm.

Sherried Hard Sauce

½ cup margarine or butter, softened
1 cup powdered sugar
1 tablespoon sherry or brandy

Beat margarine in small bowl on high speed about 5 minutes or until fluffy and light in color. Gradually beat in powdered sugar until smooth. Blend in sherry. Refrigerate about 1 hour or until chilled.

PER SERVING: Calories 555; Protein 5 g; Carbohydrate 89 g; Fat 21 g; Cholesterol 25 mg; Sodium 485 mg

Make Your Own Steamer

Plum Pudding Steamer

A steamer can be improvised using a Dutch oven or a large saucepan with a tight-fitting cover. Place a wire rack or trivet inside to raise the mold about 1 inch above the bottom of the pan.

Cranberry-Orange Bread

5
Festive Breads

Cranberry-Orange Bread

2 cups all-puprose flour
¾ cup sugar
1½ teaspoons baking powder
½ teaspoon salt
½ teaspoon baking soda
¼ cup butter or margarine, softened
1 tablespoon grated orange peel
¾ cup orange juice
1 egg
1 cup fresh or frozen (thawed and
   drained) cranberries, chopped
½ cup chopped nuts

Heat oven to 350°. Grease bottom only of loaf pan, 8½ × 4½ × 2½ or 9 × 5 × 3 inches. Mix flour, sugar, baking powder, salt and baking soda; stir in butter until mixture is crumbly. Stir in orange peel, orange juice and egg just until moistened; stir in cranberries and nuts. Spread in pan. Bake 8-inch loaf 1 hour 15 minutes, 9-inch loaf 55 to 65 minutes, or until wooden pick inserted in center comes out clean; cool 5 minutes. Loosen sides of loaf from pan; remove from pan. Cool completely before slicing.

1 loaf, 24 slices

PER SLICE: Calories 110; Protein 2 g; Carbohydrate 16 g; Fat 4 g; Cholesterol 10 mg; Sodium 110 mg

Pumpkin Bread

2⅔ cups sugar
⅔ cup shortening
4 eggs
1 can (16 ounces) pumpkin (2 cups)
⅔ cup water
3⅓ cups all-purpose flour
2 teaspoons baking soda
1½ teaspoons salt
½ teaspoon baking powder
1 teaspoon ground cinnamon
1 teaspoon ground cloves
⅔ cup coarsely chopped nuts
⅔ cup raisins

Heat oven to 350°. Grease bottoms only of two loaf pans, 9 × 5 × 3 inches, or three loaf pans, 8½ × 4½ × 2½ inches. Mix sugar and shortening in large bowl. Mix in eggs, pumpkin and water. Blend in flour, baking soda, salt, baking powder, cinnamon and cloves. Stir in nuts and raisins. Pour into pans. Bake about 1 hour 10 minutes or until wooden pick inserted in center comes out clean; cool 5 minutes. Loosen sides of loaves from pans; remove from pans. Cool completely before slicing.

2 loaves, 24 slices per loaf

PER SLICE: Calories 120; Protein 2 g; Carbohydrate 20 g; Fat 4 g; Cholesterol 20 mg; Sodium 110 mg

Banana Bread

Ripe bananas freeze easily. Mash, adding 1 tablespoon lemon juice for each cup of bananas to prevent darkening. For this recipe, freeze in 1½-cup quantities.

1¼ cups sugar
½ cup margarine or butter, softened
2 eggs
1½ cups mashed ripe bananas (3 to 4 medium)
½ cup buttermilk
1 teaspoon vanilla
2½ cups all-purpose flour
1 teaspoon baking soda
1 teaspoon salt
1 cup chopped nuts, if desired

Place oven rack in lowest position. Heat oven to 350°. Grease bottoms only of 2 loaf pans, 8½ × 4½ × 2½ inches, or 1 loaf pan, 9 × 5 × 3 inches. Mix sugar and margarine in large bowl. Stir in eggs until well blended. Add bananas, buttermilk and vanilla. Beat until smooth. Stir in remaining ingredients except nuts just until moistened. Stir in nuts. Pour into pans. Bake 8-inch loaves about 1 hour, 9-inch loaf about 1 hour 15 minutes or until wooden pick inserted in center comes out clean. Cool 5 minutes. Loosen sides of loaves from pans; remove from pans. Cool completely before slicing. Wrap tightly and store at room temperature up to 4 days, or refrigerate up to 10 days.

2 loaves (24 slices)

TO MICROWAVE: Grease 12-cup microwavable bundt cake dish generously. Prepare batter as directed. Pour into dish. Microwave uncovered on high 12 to 14 minutes, rotating dish ¼ turn every 4 minutes, until top springs back when touched lightly. Let stand on heatproof surface (not on wire rack) 10 minutes. Remove from dish; cool.

CHOCOLATE-PEANUT BANANA BREAD: Substitute ½ cup semisweet chocolate chips and ½ cup chopped peanuts for the chopped nuts.

MACADAMIA-COCONUT BANANA BREAD: Substitute 1 can (5 ounces) macadamia nuts, chopped and toasted, and ½ cup flaked coconut for the chopped nuts.

PER SERVING: Calories 85; Protein 1 g; Carbohydrate 12 g; Fat 4 g; Cholesterol 10 mg; Sodium 95 mg

Raspberry-Marzipan Coffee Cake

Streusel (right)
2 cups all-purpose flour
¾ cup sugar
¼ cup margarine or butter, softened
1 cup milk
2 teaspoons baking powder
1 teaspoon vanilla
½ teaspoon salt
1 egg
1 package (3½ ounces) almond paste, finely chopped
1 cup fresh or unsweetened frozen (thawed) raspberries

Heat oven to 350°. Prepare Streusel. Grease square pan, 9 × 9 × 2 inches. Beat all ingredients except almond paste, raspberries and Streusel in medium bowl on low speed 30 seconds. Beat on medium speed 2 minutes, scraping bowl occasionally.

Spread half of the batter in pan. Sprinkle with half each of the almond paste, raspberries and Streusel. Repeat layers. Bake about 50 minutes or until wooden pick inserted in center comes out clean. **1 coffee cake (12 pieces)**

Streusel

- ¼ **cup firm margarine or butter**
- ⅓ **cup all-purpose flour**
- ¼ **cup sugar**
- ⅓ **cup slivered almonds**

Cut margarine into flour and sugar until crumbly. Stir in nuts.

RASPBERRY-CHOCOLATE COFFEE CAKE: Substitute 1 package (6 ounces) semisweet chocolate chips (1 cup) for the almond paste.

PER SERVING: Calories 290; Protein 5 g; Carbohydrate 40 g; Fat 13 g; Cholesterol 25 mg; Sodium 265 mg

Sour Cream Coffee Cake

- **Apple-Nut Filling (right) or Brown Sugar Filling (right)**
- 1½ **cups sugar**
- ¾ **cup margarine or butter, softened**
- 3 **eggs**
- 1½ **teaspoons vanilla**
- 3 **cups all-purpose flour or whole wheat flour**
- 1½ **teaspoons baking powder**
- 1½ **teaspoons baking soda**
- ¾ **teaspoon salt**
- 1½ **cups sour cream**
- **Glaze (right)**

Heat oven to 350°. Grease tube pan, 10 × 4 inches, 12-cup bundt cake pan or 2 loaf pans, 9 × 5 × 3 inches. Prepare one of the fillings; reserve. Beat sugar, margarine, eggs and vanilla in large bowl on medium speed 2 minutes, scraping bowl occasionally. Beat in flour, baking powder, baking soda and salt alternately with sour cream on low speed.

For tube or bundt cake pan, spread one-third of the batter (about 2 cups) in pan. Sprinkle with one-third of the filling. Repeat 2 times. For loaf pans, spread one-fourth of the batter (about 1½ cups) in each pan. Sprinkle each with one-fourth of the filling. Repeat layers.

Bake about 1 hour for tube pan or bundt cake pan, about 45 minutes for loaf pans, or until wooden pick inserted near center comes out clean. Cool slightly; remove from pan. Cool 10 minutes. Drizzle with Glaze.

1 coffee cake (16 slices)

Apple-Nut Filling

- 1½ **cups chopped apples**
- ⅓ **cup packed brown sugar**
- 2 **tablespoons margarine or butter**
- 1 **tablespoon all-purpose flour**
- ¼ **teaspoon ground nutmeg**
- ⅛ **teaspoon salt**
- ½ **cup finely chopped nuts**

Cook all ingredients except nuts over medium heat, stirring constantly, until apples are tender. Stir in nuts.

Brown Sugar Filling

- ½ **cup packed brown sugar**
- ½ **cup finely chopped nuts**
- 1½ **teaspoons ground cinnamon**

Mix all ingredients.

Glaze

- ½ **cup powdered sugar**
- ¼ **teaspoon vanilla**
- 1 **to 2 teaspoons milk**

Mix all ingredients until smooth.

PER SERVING: Calories 355; Protein 5 g; Carbohydrate 47 g; Fat 17 g; Cholesterol 60 mg; Sodium 375 mg

Blueberry Buckle Coffee Cake

Blueberry Buckle Coffee Cake

A "buckle" coffeecake buckles and cracks as it bakes.

2 cups all-purpose flour
¾ cup sugar
2½ teaspoons baking powder
¾ teapsoon salt
¼ cup shortening
¾ cup milk
1 egg
2 cups fresh or frozen (thawed and drained) blueberries
Crumb Topping (below)
Glaze (below)

Heat oven to 375°. Grease square pan, 9 × 9 × 2 inches, or round pan, 9 × 1½ inches. Blend flour, sugar, baking powder, salt, shortening, milk and egg; beat 30 seconds. Carefully stir in blueberries. Spread batter in pan; sprinkle with Crumb Topping. Bake 45 to 50 minutes or until wooden pick inserted in center comes out clean. Drizzle with Glaze. Serve warm.

9 servings

Crumb Topping

½ cup sugar
⅓ cup all-purpose flour
¼ cup butter or margarine, softened
½ teaspoon ground cinnamon

Mix all ingredients until crumbly.

Glaze

½ cup powdered sugar
¼ teaspoon vanilla
1½ to 2 teaspoons hot water

Mix all ingredients until of drizzling consistency.

PER SERVING: Calories 390; Protein 5 g; Carbohydrate 65 g; Fat 12 g; Cholesterol 40 mg; Sodium 340 mg

Orange-Currant Scones

Scones come from Scotland and are often cooked on a griddle. Here they are baked for ease—but not lack of flavor!

½ cup currants
⅓ cup margarine or butter
1¾ cups all-purpose flour
3 tablespoons sugar
2½ teaspoons baking powder
¼ teaspoon salt
1 tablespoon grated orange peel
1 egg, beaten
4 to 6 tablespoons half-and-half
1 egg white, beaten

Heat oven to 400°. Soak currants in warm water for 10 minutes to soften; drain. Cut margarine into flour, sugar, baking powder and salt with pastry blender until mixture resembles fine crumbs. Stir in orange peel, egg, currants and just enough half-and-half until dough leaves side of bowl.

Turn dough onto lightly floured surface. Knead lightly 10 times. Divide dough into 2 parts. Roll or pat into two 6-inch circles about ½ inch thick. Place on ungreased cookie sheet; brush with beaten egg white. Bake 10 to 12 minutes or until golden brown. Immediately remove from cookie sheet. Cut into wedges to serve.

about 20 scones

PER SERVING: Calories 100; Protein 2 g; Carbohydrate 13 g; Fat 4 g; Cholesterol 10 mg; Sodium 120 mg

Overnight Pecan Rolls

These are great to make on Christmas Eve, then pop into the oven for warm, fresh rolls on Christmas.

3½ to 4 cups all-purpose flour
⅓ cup granulated sugar
1 teaspoon salt
2 packages active dry yeast
1 cup very warm milk (120° to 130°)
⅓ cup butter or margarine, softened
1 egg
1 cup packed brown sugar
½ cup butter or margarine
¼ cup dark corn syrup
¾ cup pecan halves
2 tablespoons butter or margarine, softened
½ cup chopped pecans
2 tablespoons granulated sugar
2 tablespoons packed brown sugar
1 teaspoon ground cinnamon

Mix 2 cups of the flour, ⅓ cup granulated sugar, the salt and yeast in large bowl. Add milk, ⅓ cup butter and the egg. Beat on low speed 1 minute, scraping bowl frequently. Beat on medium speed 1 minute, scraping bowl frequently. Stir in enough remaining flour, 1 cup at a time, to make dough easy to handle.

Turn dough onto lightly floured surface; knead about 5 minutes or until smooth and elastic. Place in greased bowl; turn greased side up. Cover and let rise in warm place about 1 hour 30 minutes or until double. (Dough is ready if indentation remains when touched.)

Grease rectangular pan, 13 × 9 × 2 inches. Heat 1 cup brown sugar and ½ cup butter to boiling, stirring constantly; remove from heat. Stir in corn syrup; cool 5 minutes. Pour into pan. Sprinkle with pecan halves.

Punch down dough. Flatten with hands or rolling pin into rectangle, 15 × 10 inches; spread with 2 tablespoons butter. Mix chopped pecans, 2 tablespoons granulated sugar, 2 tablespoons brown sugar and the cinnamon. Sprinkle evenly over rectangle. Roll up tightly, beginning at 15-inch side. Pinch edge of dough into roll to seal. Stretch and shape to make even.

Cut roll into fifteen 1-inch slices. Place slightly apart in pan. Wrap pan tightly with heavy-duty aluminum foil. Refrigerate at least 12 hours but no longer than 48 hours. (To bake immediately, do not wrap. Let rise in warm place about 30 minutes or until double. Bake as directed below.)

Heat oven to 350°. Bake uncovered 30 to 35 minutes or until golden brown. Invert immediately on heatproof serving plate or tray. Let pan remain a minute so caramel can drizzle over rolls. **15 rolls**

PER SERVING: Calories 400; Protein 5 g; Carbohydrate 52 g; Fat 19 g; Cholesterol 45 mg; Sodium 250 mg

Brown Sugar Muffins

1 cup quick-cooking oats
½ cup milk
¾ cup packed brown sugar
¼ cup margarine or butter, melted
1 egg
1 cup all-purpose flour
½ cup chopped walnuts
2 teaspoons baking powder

Heat oven to 400°. Grease 12 medium muffin cups, 2½ × 1¼ inches. Mix oats, milk and brown sugar in large bowl; let stand 5 minutes. Add margarine and egg; blend well. Stir in remaining ingredients just until moistened. Fill muffin cups two-thirds full. Bake 15 to 20 minutes or until wooden pick inserted in center comes out clean. **12 muffins**

PER SERVING: Calories 195; Protein 3 g; Carbohydrate 28 g; Fat 8 g; Cholesterol 20 mg; Sodium 125 mg

Muffins of Any Size

Make muffins any size you like! If your recipe has a filling or topping, you might need more or less of it, depending on the size muffins you make.

Baking time will also vary based on the size. Smaller muffins will take 5 to 10 minutes less to bake than medium muffins, and larger muffins will take 5 to 10 minutes longer.

If your recipes make 12 medium muffins, you'll get:

Small Muffins
Use: 1¾-inch muffin cups
Yield: About 36 muffins

Large Muffins
Use: 3 × 1½-inch muffin cups
Yield: About 8 muffins

Jumbo Muffins
Use: 6-ounce custard cups
Yield: About 4 muffins

Make-ahead Raisin Brioche

1 package active dry yeast
3 tablespoons warm water
2 teaspoons sugar
3½ cups all-purpose flour
½ cup sugar
1 teaspoon ground cinnamon
½ teaspoon salt
¾ cup cold margarine or butter, cut up
⅓ cup milk
3 eggs
1½ cups golden raisins
1 egg white

Mix yeast, water and 2 teaspoons sugar in small bowl; set aside. Place flour, ½ cup sugar, the cinnamon and salt in food processor; cover and process until mixed. Add margarine; process until well blended.

Whisk milk and eggs into yeast mixture; slowly add to flour mixture and process until well blended. Stir in raisins. (Dough will be sticky.) Turn dough out onto well-floured surface. Knead 1 minute until dough is smooth, adding more flour if necessary. Place in large greased bowl; cover tightly. Let dough rise in warm place 40 minutes.

Grease 12 large muffin cups, 3½ × 1½ inches. Punch dough down. Using about ¼ cup dough each, make 12 balls; place in muffin cups. Using about 1 tablespoon dough each, make 12 smaller balls; place on top of each large ball. Cover and refrigerate overnight.

Remove rolls from refrigerator. Let rise in warm place 40 to 45 minutes or until almost double in size. Heat oven to 350°. Uncover; beat egg white; brush rolls with egg white. Bake 22 to 26 minutes until golden brown. **12 brioches**

PER SERVING: Calories 355; Protein 6 g; Carbohydrate 53 g; Fat 13 g; Cholesterol 55 mg; Sodium 250 mg

Saint Lucia Crown

1⅙ to ⅛ teaspoon crushed saffron*
½ cup lukewarm milk (scalded then cooled)
2 packages active dry yeast
½ cup warm water (105° to 115°)
½ cup sugar
1 teaspoon salt
2 eggs, beaten
¼ cup margarine or butter, softened
4½ to 5 cups all-purpose flour
½ cup cut-up citron
¼ cup chopped blanched almonds
1 tablespoon grated lemon peel
Powdered Sugar Glaze (right)
Candied cherries

Stir saffron into milk. Dissolve yeast in warm water in large bowl. Stir in saffron-milk, sugar, salt, eggs, margarine and 2½ cups of the flour. Beat until smooth. Stir in citron, almonds, lemon peel and enough remaining flour to make dough easy to handle.

Turn dough onto lightly floured surface; knead until smooth and elastic, about 10 minutes. Place in greased bowl; turn greased side up. Cover; let rise in warm place until double, about 1 hour 30 minutes. (Dough is ready if indentation remains when touched.)

Punch down dough; cut off one-third of the dough for top braid and reserve. Divide remaining dough into 3 equal parts; roll each part into 25-inch strip. Place close together on greased cookie sheet. Braid strips; shape into circle and pinch ends to seal.

Divide reserved dough into 3 equal parts; roll each part into 16-inch strip. Place close together on another greased cookie sheet. Braid strips; shape into circle and pinch ends to seal. Cover both braids; let rise until double, about 45 minutes.

*2 or 3 drops of yellow food color can be substituted for the saffron.

Heat oven to 375°. Bake until golden brown, 20 to 25 minutes. When cool, make holes for 5 candles in small braid. Drizzle both braids with Powdered Sugar Glaze; garnish with cherries. Insert candles. Place small braid on large braid.

18 servings

Powdered Sugar Glaze

Mix 1 cup powdered sugar and 3 to 4 teaspoons water until smooth and of desired consistency.

LUCIA BUNS: When ready to shape dough, cut into pieces about 2½ inches in diameter. Shape each piece into 12-inch roll; form into tightly coiled "S" shape. Place a raisin in center of each coil. Place on greased cookie sheet. Brush tops lightly with margarine or butter; let rise until double, about 45 minutes. Bake until golden brown, about 15 minutes.

about 1½ dozen buns

PER SERVING OR BUN: Calories 220; Protein 5 g; Carbohydrate 41 g; Fat 4 g; Cholesterol 25 mg; Sodium 170 mg

Holiday Braid

1 package active dry yeast
¼ cup warm water (105° to 115°)
¾ cup lukewarm milk (scalded then cooled)
¼ cup sugar
¼ cup shortening
1 teaspoon salt
1 egg
½ cup raisins
½ cup chopped almonds
1 teaspoon grated lemon peel
⅛ teaspoon ground mace
3½ to 3¾ cups all-purpose flour
1 egg yolk
2 tablespoons cold water
Powdered Sugar Glaze (above)

Dissolve yeast in warm water in large bowl. Stir in milk, sugar, shortening, salt, egg, raisins, almonds, lemon peel, mace and 1¾ cups of the flour. Beat until smooth. Stir in enough remaining flour to make dough easy to handle.

Turn dough onto lightly floured surface; knead until smooth and elastic, about 5 minutes. Place in greased bowl; turn greased side up. Cover; let rise in warm place until double, about 1½ hours. (Dough is ready if indentation remains when touched.)

Punch down dough. Divide into 4 equal parts; roll 3 of the parts into 14-inch strips. Place close together on lightly greased cookie sheet. Braid loosely; pinch ends together and fold under. Divide remaining part into 3 pieces and roll each into 12-inch strip. Braid strips; place on large braid. Cover and let rise until double, 45 to 60 minutes.

Heat oven to 350°. Mix egg yolk and cold water; brush on coffee cake. Bake until golden brown, 30 to 40 minutes. Spread with Powdered Sugar Glaze while warm.   **24 servings.**

PER SERVING: Calories 150; Protein 3 g; Carbohydrate 25 g; Fat 4 g; Cholesterol 20 mg; Sodium 95 mg

Kris Kringle Stollen

3½ cups all-purpose flour
½ cup sugar
½ teaspoon salt
1 package active dry yeast
¾ cup very warm water (120° to 130°)
½ cup butter or margarine, softened
3 eggs
1 egg, separated
½ cup chopped blanched almonds
¼ cup diced citron
¼ cup cut-up candied cherries
¼ cup raisins
1 tablespoon grated lemon peel
Butter or margarine, softened
1 tablespoon water
Glaze (right) or powdered sugar

Mix 1¾ cups of the flour, the sugar, salt and yeast in large bowl. Add water, ½ cup butter, the eggs and egg yolk. Beat on low speed 1 minute, scraping bowl frequently. Beat on medium speed 10 minutes, scraping bowl frequently. Stir in remaining flour, the almonds, citron, cherries, raisins and lemon peel. Scrape batter from side of bowl. Cover and let rise in warm place 1 hour 30 minutes to 2 hours or until double.

Stir down batter by beating about 25 strokes. Cover tightly and store in refrigerator at least 8 hours.

Grease cookie sheet. Turn dough onto well-floured surface; turn to coat with flour. Divide into halves. Flatten each half with hands or rolling pin into oval, 10 × 7 inches. Spread with butter. Fold lengthwise in half; press only folded edge firmly. Place on cookie sheet with folded sides toward center. Beat egg white and 1 tablespoon water; brush over ovals. Let rise 45 to 60 minutes or until double.

Heat oven to 375°. Bake 20 to 25 minutes or until golden brown. Spread with Glaze while warm; decorate with almonds, pieces of citron and candied cherry halves if desired, or sprinkle tops with powdered sugar.

                2 coffee cakes, 12 slices each

Glaze

1½ cups powdered sugar
½ teaspoon vanilla
2 to 3 tablespoons water

Mix all ingredients until smooth and spreadable.

PER SLICE: Calories 205; Protein 3 g; Carbohydrate 30 g; Fat 8 g; Cholesterol 50 mg; Sodium 100 mg

Fruited Christmas Wreath

2 packages active dry yeast
½ cup warm water (105° to 115°)
1¼ cups buttermilk
½ cup granulated sugar
½ cup margarine or butter, softened
2 eggs
2 teaspoons baking powder
2 teaspoons salt
5½ cups all-purpose flour
1 cup cut-up mixed candied fruit
½ cup chopped pecans
1 tablespoon grated lemon peel
½ cup powdered sugar
1 tablespoon milk

Dissolve yeast in warm water in large mixer bowl. Add buttermilk, granulated sugar, margarine, eggs, baking powder, salt and 2½ cups of the flour. Beat on low speed, scraping bowl constantly, 30 seconds. Beat on medium speed, scraping bowl occasionally, 2 minutes. Stir in remaining flour, the candied fruit, pecans and lemon peel. (Dough will be soft and slightly sticky.)

Turn dough onto well-floured surface; knead until smooth and elastic, about 5 minutes. Roll into strip, 24 × 6 inches. Cut into 3 strips, 24 × 2 inches. Place close together on greased cookie sheet. Braid strips; shape into circle and pinch ends to seal. Cover; let rise in warm place until double, about 1 hour. (Dough is ready if indentation remains when touched.)

Heat oven to 375°. Bake until golden brown, about 30 minutes. Mix powdered sugar and milk; drizzle over wreath while warm. Decorate with green and red candied cherries if desired.

1 large coffee cake, 32 slices

NOTE: For two small wreaths, divide dough after kneading into halves. Roll each half into rectangle, 18 × 3 inches. Cut into 3 strips, each 18 × 1 inch. Continue as directed—except bake 20 to 30 minutes. Omit powdered sugar and milk and brush with softened margarine or butter if desired.

PER SLICE; Calories 165; Protein 3 g; Carbohydrate 27 g; Fat 5 g; Cholesterol 15 mg; Sodium 220 mg

CHRISTMAS TREE BREAD: Omit candied fruit, pecans, lemon peel, powered sugar and milk. Divide dough into halves; shape 1 half at a time into seventeen 2-inch balls. Form tree shape with balls in rows of 5, 4, 3, 2, 1 on lightly greased cookie sheet. Roll remaining 2 balls together for trunk of tree. Cover; let rise in warm place 1 hour. Bake until golden brown, 20 to 25 minutes. Remove from cookie sheets and cool.

Beat 2 cups powdered sugar, 2 to 3 tablespoons water or milk and 1 teaspoon vanilla until smooth. Decorate trees with frosting. Trim with candied fruits.

2 coffee cakes, 16 slices each

Christmas Tree Bread

Snowman Buns

Snowman Buns are an adaptation of a New Year's bread that originated in St. Albans, England. Tradition has it that the little breads were called "Pope Ladies" for the legendary Popess Joan of A.D. 858.

1 package active dry yeast
¾ cup warm water (105° to 115°)
⅓ cup sugar
¼ cup shortening
2 eggs
2 teaspoons ground nutmeg, if desired
1 teaspoon salt
3½ cups all-purpose flour
60 currants
1 egg, slightly beaten

Dissolve yeast in warm water in large mixer bowl. Add sugar, shortening, 2 eggs, the nutmeg, salt and 2 cups of the flour. Beat on low speed, scraping bowl constantly, 30 seconds. Beat on medium speed, scraping bowl occasionally, 2 minutes. Stir in remaining flour until smooth. Cover; let rise in warm place until double, about 45 minutes. (Dough is ready if indentation remains when touched with floured finger.)

Stir down dough by beating 25 strokes. Turn onto well-floured surface; cut into 12 equal parts (each part will make 1 snowman). Shape one-half of each part into 4-inch oval for the body. Shape one-half of the remaining dough into ball for the head. Press in tiny piece of dough for nose. Shape remaining dough into 4-inch roll and cut into halves for arms

Arrange snowmen about 3 inches apart on greased cookie sheet. Let rise until double, about 45 minutes. Press in 2 currants for eyes and 3 for buttons. Heat oven to 350°. Brush snowmen with beaten egg. Bake until golden brown, about 15 minutes. Decorate with Creamy Decorators' Frosting (page 2) if desired.

1 dozen buns

PER BUN: Calories 210; Protein 5 g; Carbohydrate 35 g; Fat 6 g; Cholesterol 55 mg; Sodium 190 mg

Marvelous Mini Loaves

You can bake quick-bread batter in miniature loaf pans, muffin pans, small cake molds or other baking pans. Pumpkin Bread (page 73) and Banana Bread (page 74) are good choices. Use these handy guidelines to turn your favorite fruit-and-nut bread into delightful little morsels!

• Measure the volume of pans by filling them to the top with water, then pouring the water into a measuring cup.

• Dry the pans well and grease them generously. Grease the bottoms only of muffin cups and miniature loaf pans. Thoroughly grease other pans, such as small cake molds.

• Spoon the batter into greased pans. Refer to the chart below to determine how much batter to spoon into each pan.

• Bake at 350° until a toothpick inserted in the center comes out clean. Use the chart below to determine approximate baking times. The dimensions and shapes of the pans will affect the baking time.

• Let the breads cool for a few minutes, then loosen the edges of the breads from the pans and carefully remove them from the pans. Cool completely on a wire rack.

Mini Loaves Baking Chart

APPROXIMATE PAN VOLUME	AMOUNT OF BATTER	APPROXIMATE BAKING TIME
⅓ cup	¼ cup	15 to 20 minutes
½ cup	⅓ cup	15 to 20 minutes
⅔ to ¾ cup	½ cup	25 to 35 minutes
1 cup	¾ cup	35 to 40 minutes

METRIC CONVERSION GUIDE

U.S. UNITS	CANADIAN METRIC	AUSTRALIAN METRIC
Volume		
1/4 teaspoon	1 mL	1 ml
1/2 teaspoon	2 mL	2 ml
1 teaspoon	5 mL	5 ml
1 tablespoon	15 mL	20 ml
1/4 cup	50 mL	60 ml
1/3 cup	75 mL	80 ml
1/2 cup	125 mL	125 ml
2/3 cup	150 mL	170 ml
3/4 cup	175 mL	190 ml
1 cup	250 mL	250 ml
1 quart	1 liter	1 liter
1 1/2 quarts	1.5 liter	1.5 liter
2 quarts	2 liters	2 liters
2 1/2 quarts	2.5 liters	2.5 liters
3 quarts	3 liters	3 liters
4 quarts	4 liters	4 liters
Weight		
1 ounce	30 grams	30 grams
2 ounces	55 grams	60 grams
3 ounces	85 grams	90 grams
4 ounces (1/4 pound)	115 grams	125 grams
8 ounces (1/2 pound)	225 grams	225 grams
16 ounces (1 pound)	455 grams	500 grams
1 pound	455 grams	1/2 kilogram

Measurements

Inches	Centimeters
1	2.5
2	5.0
3	7.5
4	10.0
5	12.5
6	15.0
7	17.5
8	20.5
9	23.0
10	25.5
11	28.0
12	30.5
13	33.0
14	35.5
15	38.0

Temperatures

Fahrenheit	Celsius
32°	0°
212°	100°
250°	120°
275°	140°
300°	150°
325°	160°
350°	180°
375°	190°
400°	200°
425°	220°
450°	230°
475°	240°
500°	260°

NOTE
The recipes in this cookbook have not been developed or tested using metric measures. When converting recipes to metric, some variations in quality may be noted.

Index

Page numbers in *italics* indicate photographs.